"Nobody interested in the 1942-45 War in the Pacific should neglect Leon Cooper's book, which asks vital questions about the destructive, unended rivalry between the commands of General MacArthur and Admiral Nimitz, about lessons not learned from slaughter at Tarawa and Peleliu, about the failure of knowledge from the Manhattan Project to alter island-hopping after the Marianas Islands, and about dependence on the unreliable B-29s that could have spared one or more from the trio of Marianas, Iwo Jima and Okinawa."

> —Carl Woodring, former Chairman, Department of English, Columbia University and U.S. Naval officer veteran of the Pacific War.

"Leon Cooper's first battle did not earn the name of "Bloody Tarawa" because things went well. He will tell you as he told me that the enemy was brave—if brutal—and that the plans laid by his own commanders didn't work out as written. It is a testament to the assault boat commanders' tenacity, basic skills, and ability to improvise that helped US Marines to victory in a battle that would cause mothers of the fallen to call for the firing of Admiral Nimitz, the man they held responsible for killing their sons at Tarawa.

Yet Bloody Tarawa had only happened in November of 1943. Victory in the Pacific would be years in coming. In the mean time, many other well-defended islands would have to be assaulted at the cost of many US lives before the final bomber offensive against Japan could be unleashed to end the war.

Leon Cooper now asks: Was there another way? Read his intriguing and informed impressions of the Pacific War and reach your own conclusions."

> —Michael Puttre, Former Editor-in-Ch
> "JED, *Journal of Electronic Defense.*" 1
> award-winning documentary, "Nagasa

"I've reread "War Plan Orange—Tarawa the Crucible" and find your narrative very stimulating and thought-provoking. The retrospective view of Pacific battles reveals cases where bypass would have been a better choice than attack…We learned the hard way."

> —Donald K Allen, Author, *Tarawa—the Aftermath*

The War in the Pacific:
A Retrospective

Leon Cooper

ISBN 13: 978-0-9790584-0-0
ISBN 10: 0-9790584-0-6

Published by 90 Day Wonder Publishing

Design and layout by Selfpublishing.com

Printed in the United States of America

www.warinpacific.net

About the Cover

On a personal note ...

The author and many others probably owe our lives to the pilots shown in the photograph.

These pilots, from the aircraft carrier USS Lexington, are celebrating their victory over a flight of Japanese planes they had destroyed in aerial combat. The Japanese planes, based in the nearby Marshall Islands, had been en route to Tarawa to bomb and strafe the landing forces. They were intercepted by the Lexington pilots just as they neared Tarawa. None of the Japanese planes got through. As a landing craft Naval officer, I was leading a wave of Higgins Boats carrying more than a hundred Marines into the beaches of Betio, in Tarawa, on the first day of that battle.

By Leon Cooper

An Invitation to Learning—An Instructor's Manual

90 Day Wonder—Darkness Remembered
        (A book with Don Tait)

90 Day Wonder (A Screenplay with Don Tait)

Acknowledgements

FIRST AND FOREMOST, OUR nation owes a great debt to all who took part in a war whose victorious outcome literally saved our civilization. It is the sergeants, the petty officers, the junior officers—and especially the rank and file—who were in the front lines; all these were the vital difference between defeat and victory. Another acknowledgement is long overdue: our nation needs to acknowledge, with shame, those who fell in battles that should not have been fought, or who died in battles led by commanders who were incompetent, or worse. I wrote this book to explain how these tragic events took place.

My thanks to my editor, Patricia Fry, who helped me keep my sentences to less than a page in length; to my brother, Professor William W. Cooper, who insisted that my book was "important," and encouraged me to keep writing. My thanks to my fellow warrior, Carl Woodring, also a Naval officer during the Pacific War, whose suggestions I adopted because they will keep me from being sued. My thanks, finally, to Carol Cavella and her husband Joe, for helping me put the book together.

CONTENTS

Of the events of the war I have not ventured to speak from any chance information, nor according to any notion of my own; I have described nothing but what I either saw myself or learned from others of whom I made the most careful and particular inquiry. But if he who desires to have before his eyes a true picture of the events which have happened, and of the like events which may be expected to happen hereafter in the order of human things shall pronounce what I have written to be useful, then I shall be satisfied.

—Thucydides, *The Peloponnesian War*

Introduction

I WAS A LANDING craft officer with the U.S. Navy during World War II and took part in six invasions of Japanese-held islands. There were other invasions in the Pacific, of course, in which I did not take part. However, I knew men who were in some of those battles and they shared their experiences with me. This book includes not only my own true accounts, but also the stories of others, thus it is based on original sources.

Much has been written about the War in the Pacific by able historians. I've consulted their books, but I don't believe that some of my questions have been properly dealt with. In this book I address these questions from the point of view of a participant, not a historian. And, as a participant, I have challenged the judgment of those who decided which battles were to be fought and when. No doubt, some of my opinions will be regarded as unorthodox, but they are opinions based on my experiences. I saw firsthand the disastrous consequences of "orthodoxy." Throughout these pages I make harsh judgments about some of our nation's top war leaders. By way of brief explanation here: those whom I have taken to task made mistakes of monumental proportions, causing untold thousands of U.S. casualties. Many of these mistakes arose from the seeming unwillingness of those in command to prepare and to use alternate strategies to meet changing conditions. These mistakes were almost criminal.

I have long had questions about some of the battles occurring during the War in the Pacific. Was "Island-Hopping" the most effective, and the quickest, way of defeating the Japanese? Why were some of the Japanese strongholds bypassed? And yet other redoubts, not critical in Japan's ultimate defeat, were assaulted with heavy U.S. losses. Did we learn anything as we advanced from one invasion to the next, especially in reducing our casualties? Was it unusual for those B-29 crews to ditch in the ocean near our transport group so their air crews could be rescued as we steamed en route to the invasion of Iwo Jima? Was there something radically wrong with these big planes?

A number of historians have written about the inter-service rivalries that dominated actions in the War in the Pacific. Indeed, two wars were being waged: the one against the Japanese, the other between the services. In this book I show that the war between the services caused far more harm than has been recognized—especially in the number of casualties that it produced. A vainglorious General MacArthur and a stiff-necked Admiral Nimitz were the two primary combatants—each trying to outgame the other. While railing against the Navy's "Cabal"[1]—as MacArthur repeatedly called it—the General tried to proselytize William ("Bull") Halsey, Nimitz's most senior Admiral, importuning him to "Come with me and I'll make you greater than Nelson ever dreamed of being."[2] Not one to be outdone by MacArthur, Nimitz would allow the General command over *his* admirals and *his* ships only under rigorously defined conditions. This would be the game these two Senior Commanders would play all during the Pacific War.

By far the greatest fault, however, lay with FDR, the Commander in Chief's, incredible failure to put a stop to the rivalry. Unfortunately, this one-upmanship behavior continued throughout the war with Japan, even though FDR must have been aware of the magnitude of the problems this divided command was creating. Typical of the murky, muddled chain of command structure was the language that appears in SOPAC COMMAND ORDER (South Pacific Command) in connection with the New Guinea/Solomons campaign: "Admiral Halsey's operations are under General MacArthur's strategic direction. Halsey is subordinate administratively and logistically to Admiral Nimitz."[3] (One must wonder what Halsey was supposed to do had Nimitz and MacArthur disagreed on any matter of substance during that campaign).

If, early in the Pacific war, FDR had declared unequivocally who was in sole command in that theatre, the many casualties resulting from this rivalry would have been avoided. Instead, late in the war, Roosevelt would compound the confused command structure in the Pacific by overruling an essential, far-reaching decision by the Joint Chiefs of Staff.[4] FDR's action would result in thousands of U.S. casualties of questionable value in the ultimate defeat of Japan—even if there had been no A-bomb. There is good reason for believing that FDR did this because he wanted the General to remain in the Pacific and not return home to compete with him for the presidency in the upcoming election.[5]

President Truman perpetuated FDR's bad judgment by allowing MacArthur, rather than, say, General George Marshall, to take center stage by presiding over the Japanese surrender ceremony aboard the USS Missouri. Nimitz, now a minor player in the drama, must have given serious thought to staying away.

War Plan Orange
Tarawa—the Crucible

War is the unfolding of miscalculations.
—Barbara Tuchman

THE WORLD, ESPECIALLY THE U.S. Navy, became aware of the prowess of the Japanese Navy after its stunning defeat of the Russian fleet in the Battle of Tsushima Strait, in 1905.[6]

The Russians lost forty-five capital ships—two-thirds of its entire fleet. There were more than 12,000 Russian casualties, including 4,830 who were killed. The Japanese losses were confined to three torpedo boats. Just 200 men were wounded, one of whom was a man named Lieutenant Isoroku Yamamoto. Later, as Commander of the Japanese Fleet, Admiral Yamamoto would plan and direct the attack upon Pearl Harbor, as part of his grand plan to defeat American, British and Dutch forces throughout the Pacific.

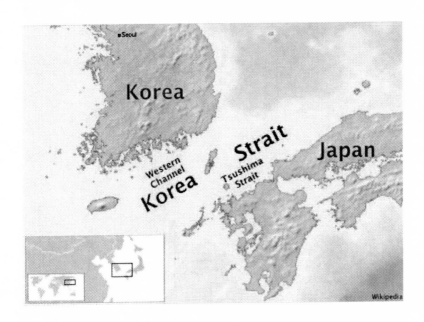

War Plan Orange—"Orange" being the U.S. Navy code for Japan—was first conceived by U.S. Navy planners in the late 1800s, following Admiral Alfred Mahan's seminal writings on *Victory Through Sea Power*. The Japanese victory in Tsushima Strait was compelling evidence to the U.S. Navy planners that America's hegemony in the Pacific was now seriously threatened. Mid-ocean bases were conceived as an integral part of War Plan Orange.[7] Certain islands in the Central Pacific were to be taken in the advance toward Japan. "Island Hopping," as it became known, was deemed to be the key to ultimate victory. War games based on Island-

Hopping were played out in the U.S. Naval War College. The game objective was to secure a series of strategically located islands in the Central Pacific, using each to advance to the next, finally occupying the defeated Japan. Remarkably, the games were based on the assumption that the Japanese would strike first, taking possession of the Philippines, then moving east.

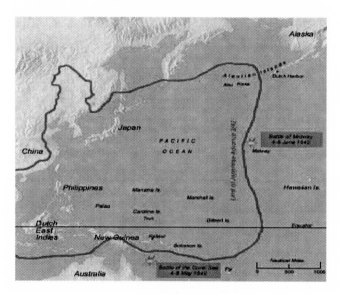

Japan's "dominance" in 1942

Japanese naval strategists, with their own version of war games, knew they had to establish strongholds in important areas of the Pacific in order to counter America's War Plan Orange.[8] Starting in the 1930s, Japan began its conquest of island groups. Combined Fleet Top Secret Operational Order No. 1, issued in November, 1941, (See Appendix "B") would accelerate these conquests to include the East Indies, the Bismarcks, Wake, the Solomons, New Britain, the Gilberts, the Marianas, in addition to island groups that the Japanese had acquired from a defeated Germany in 1918.

With the taking of New Guinea early in the war, Japan had set up a formidable defensive perimeter—one which was also intended to discourage America's will to fight. Also, Japan's planners reasoned, with America's retreat from its dominance in the Pacific, the seas would be open to allow Australia and New Zealand to become Japanese possessions. Only the Soviet Union would prevent Japan from taking control of all of Asia.

With U.S. victories in the Battle of Midway and in the Solomons, the U.S. would begin the first of its series of Island-Hopping advances toward Japan, starting with the Gilbert Islands and including the taking of Tarawa in November, 1943.[9] It would be the first assault upon a heavily defended Japanese island. This was also the first time that new types of Higgins boats and other new amphibious vessels, including DUKWs and LVTs, would be used. The tactics of "wave formations," "demarcation points," "H Hours" and all other details had been worked out in the invasion of Sicily months earlier.[10] A massive armada sailed toward the Gilberts in "Operation Galvanic." Makin, the northernmost island in the Gilberts would be taken first.[11]

Tarawa, next in the Gilberts assault, would prove to be a poor choice. Tarawa's air group, the Japanese High Command had decided before the war, was an important link in the chain of air offensive/defensive bases in the Central Pacific.[12] The Tarawa air group and the one in the nearby Marshall Islands together were the keystone of Japan's Central Pacific dominance. For that reason, the aircraft base and related facilities on Betio—the island in the Tarawa atoll where the major fighting would take place—would have a formidable defense complex such as U.S. forces had not encountered before. (Tarawa's defenses would be the pattern American invasion forces would encounter in subsequent island assaults.)

Historian Admiral Morison has described the defenses as follows: "At the corners of the island and at various other points along the shore there were coast defense guns ranging from 5.5 inch to 8 inch. Along and inside the beach were 25 field guns, 37mm and 75mm in covered emplacements, mostly in pillboxes well protected from shrapnel blasts by a thick covering of logs and sand reinforced by armor plate or concrete caps, and immune to direct hits from all but the largest guns. A number of anti-aircraft guns were located throughout the island, ranging in size from 13mm to 5.1 inch."[13]

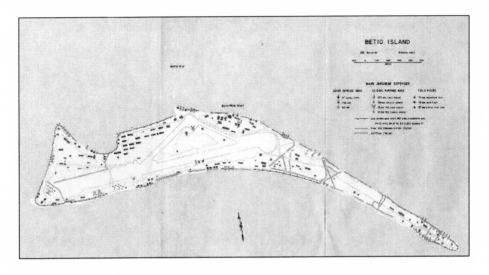

Upon viewing the Betio defense structure remains after the battle, storied Marine Corps General Holland ("Howling Mad") Smith expressed surprise that the island had been secured in just three days. After the war, Smith said, "Tarawa was a mistake." Lt. Colonel David Shoup, who was awarded the Medal of Honor for his bravery and leadership during the battle, would later wonder, "Why two nations would spend so much for so little."

Adding to these defenses was the "regiment of the 1,559 man crack 7th Sasebo Special Naval Landing Force," according to one report. There was a total of 2,600 defenders on Betio, a tiny island just two miles long and a half-mile wide. Altogether, 4,800 men were stationed there, including 2,200 construction laborers. Admiral Shibaski, the Tarawa Commander, told his garrison, "One million Americans couldn't take Tarawa in a hundred years."[14] There would be only 146 survivors—mainly Korean laborers who were part of the construction group.

After the battle, this island group became known as "Bloody Tarawa" and rightly so. U.S. reporters took photographs showing dead American Marines in tragically grotesque positions—sprawled across the seawall, lying face down in the waters lapping the beach shelf, crouching behind a palm tree stump. One man was pictured half in and half out of an LVT.

These photos were viewed at home by a shocked American public, also by an angry President Roosevelt. General Douglas MacArthur also weighed in, "These frontal attacks by the Navy, as at Tarawa, are tragic and unnecessary massacres of American lives,"[15] thundered the General to a representative of Secretary of War Stimson, who had sought MacArthur's views on the Island-Hopping strategy.[16] The General himself was not one to avoid frontal attacks. Early in the Pacific War he insisted that the Japanese "Fortress Rabaul" on New Britain should be taken. Rabaul, at its peak, had 200,000 armed forces personnel there, with the advantage of a massive defense structure and hundreds of miles of tunnels.[17] There was no way of taking it except through frontal attacks. Fortunately, the General was overruled.

In the three days of violence before final victory at Tarawa, the 2nd Division Marines suffered 3,400 casualties. With an 18,600 attacking force, this was almost a one in five casualty rate. The toll upon American forces would have been much greater had there not been a breakdown in Japanese communications. The order to "destroy the enemy transports" that were approaching their boat-launching sites was evidently not transmitted. And, fortunately for the landing forces, seventeen of the twenty Japanese planes dispatched to Tarawa from the Marshalls were destroyed by U.S. carrier pilots from the USS Lexington as they neared Betio.[18] (This is the same phtograph that appears on the cover of this book.)

Why did U.S. Naval strategists choose Tarawa? They figured that, with a base on Betio, including an airstrip, the Marshalls, the next phase in the Island-Hopping campaign, could be launched successfully.[19] Of course, nobody then in command would dare to admit publicly that the invasion of Tarawa, with such a shocking loss of lives, was to serve as a test—a crucible—for learning how amphibious operations should be conducted in later invasions. Was what happened at Tarawa worth it? On the contrary, it would hardly prove to be the model for subsequent landings, as Marine General Holland Smith himself explained to his fellow officers during a meeting on the command ship, USS Rocky Mount, just before the invasion of Guam. "We are through with atolls now. We learned to pulverize atolls, but now we are up against mountains and caves where Japs can dig in. A week from now there will be a lot of dead Marines."[20] Indeed, questions can be raised as to whether the Tarawa victory would figure materially in the ultimate defeat of Japan.

Despite its bitter Tarawa experience, the U.S. Navy High Command and others in command decided to proceed to the next step, continuing with the originally planned battle sequence. Next would be the Marshalls, then the Marianas, then Palau, then (possibly) the Philippines. Next would be either Iwo Jima or nearby Chichi Jima, also in the Bonin Islands, both part of the "Bonin Ladder." With the taking of Okinawa, the stage would be set for the invasion of Japan. All of the foregoing series of battles were planned before December 7, 1941, before dramatic changes in sea and air power had begun to unfold.[21] The question is obvious: Should not pre-1941 battle plans, especially those involving Island-Hopping, have been rigorously reviewed? There is no record that this was done, even though the type of war planned before December 7, 1941 would be an altogether different one after that date. Immediately after December 7, the U.S. Navy began to accelerate its dramatic metamorphosis from a battleship Navy to one dominated by aircraft carriers and air power. Clearly, pre-1941 plans were outdated, at least in part, resulting in the needless and tragic sacrifice of American lives.

As discussed elsewhere in this book, President Roosevelt from the outset wanted to force Japan to surrender by relying on aerial bombardment. There was minimal success with B-29 bombing raids from remote bases in China and India. For that reason, Saipan and Tinian, in the Marianas, were chosen to be the new B-29 base. These islands were within B-29 range of the Japanese home islands, especially Tokyo on Honshu. Indeed, the Marianas were taken from the Japanese less than a year after Tarawa. It would be from Tinian that B-29s took off to bomb Hiroshima and Nagasaki.[22]

Another obvious question: Why weren't the Marianas invaded after Tarawa was seized rather than delaying the action with the cautious, island-by-island takeovers? If we had taken the Marianas earlier in the war, bombing raids on Japan's cities could have begun much sooner. Similarly, what was the strategic significance of invading Palau and the Southern Philippines? How would either victory figure in the defeat of Japan? (Neither did, as will be argued elsewhere in this book.) If the Marianas had been taken earlier rather than after Tarawa, it may be claimed that the sea lanes in the Western Pacific would be exposed to Japanese air and sea attacks, hindering supplies from Hawaii to that sector. While true, it is essential to bear in mind that important and accelerated developments were getting underway while the Tarawa battle was being fought. By February, 1944, "Fortress Rabaul" on New Britain had been neutralized by the conquest of the nearby Green Islands by a force of U.S. and New Zealand troops. Later that year, photos from Admiral Mitscher's Carrier Group, Task Force

58, operating in the Western Pacific, showed that Mitscher's pilots had delivered two devastating attacks on Japan's now rapidly weakening defenses. First, flyers from Task Force 58 had destroyed more than 300 Japanese planes in air combat in the famous "Marianas Turkey Shoot." More important than the planes was the loss of Japan's most experienced pilots, many of whom, ironically, had been in the Pearl Harbor attack. Then, shortly afterward, in a two-day aerial assault, Mitscher's pilots bombed and strafed Truk, Japan's "Gibralter of the Pacific."[23]

"Fortress Rabaul" on New Britain

Japanese "Betty" bomber on Truk

During these two air strikes on Truk, more than 300,000 tons of shipping was sunk, including a number of capital ships. Hundreds of planes on the ground and in the air were destroyed by the Task Force carrier planes, winnowing more of what remained of Japanese rapidly dwindling air power. Finally, Truk's infrastructure was completely demolished by Mitscher's flyers, leaving the remaining garrison cut off from their supply route. Many on the island would ultimately die of disease or starvation.[24]

By the time Tarawa was taken, America had begun to assemble the greatest armada in the history of naval warfare. Before war's end, the U.S. Navy would have 1,471 operational ships of the line—mainly in the Pacific. They were as follows:[25] (See Appendix "A").

TYPE	NUMBER
Aircraft Carriers	146
Battleships	8
Cruisers	48
Destroyers	349
Convoy Escorts	498
Submarines	422

The list does not include the many hundreds of "ships of the train" such as tankers, supply ships, repair ships, troop transports, and other ships which are not classified as "men-of-war," or "ships of the line," in Navy parlance. Neither does the list include the many thousands of vessels of various types that were used in amphibious operations, e.g., LSTs, LCIs, LCTs, LVTs, DUKWs, LCMs, LCVPs, etc.[26]

To restate the obvious: Could a strategy conceived in the 1920s or even in the 30s have anticipated the dominant role aircraft carriers and air power would play in the war against Japan?[27] In addition to those mentioned above, other decisive victories against Japan, where aircraft carriers were also the margin of victory, included: the Battle of the Coral Sea, the Battle of Midway, the Battle of the Bismarck Sea. The cumulative effect of these American victories would produce in a reeling Japan an unwanted, but surely not an unexpected, outcome. Japan, in a last ditch defense, would make the U.S. pay dearly in blood for each invasion hereafter.

Tragically, even more American casualties were to take place in these invasions owing to the seeming unwillingness of the commanders at the scene to alter their battle plans, as will be explained later, even after they became aware of the extraordinary defense installations the Japanese had made.

The Killing Fields—Palau

Soldiers usually win the battles and generals
get the credit for them.
—*Napoleon Bonaparte*

"EXPERIENCE THE WONDERS OF Palau," rhapsodizes the blurb writer in a recent brochure, claiming that "Palau offers you the world's most beautiful tropical paradise. Palau is rated as one of the world's best diving adventures ..." And why not? "Palau has unspoiled reefs, caves and the most amazing array of marine life. Imagine the whitest beaches, the clearest waters, forests, waterfalls, and caves that have never been ravaged by man ..." And the brochure goes on to say, "Hundreds of islands abound all along this pristine archipelago."[28]

The Palau Islands

It would be difficult for a Marine of the 1st Division or a soldier of the 81st Army Division who survived the horrors of the battle for Pelelieu, in Palau, in 1944, to "imagine," to be taken in by these blandishments, or to want to return to this "paradise" where there were 10,786 U.S. casualties during a period of little more than two months of bitter combat against an entrenched Japanese defense in disease-infested jungles. The casualty rate in the battle for "Bloody Tarawa," waged a year earlier, would be exceeded here, and would be the highest rate of any amphibious invasion during the Pacific War.[29]

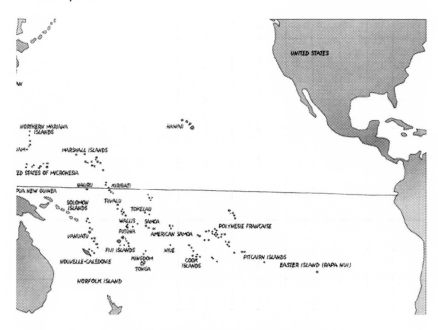

Palau—just southeast of the Philippines

The two commanders in the Pacific War, General MacArthur and Admiral Nimitz, often disagreed, but were in agreement that Palau had to be invaded.[30] MacArthur believed that Palau in Japanese hands was a potential offensive threat to his planned invasion of the nearby Philippines. And Nimitz had promised MacArthur that he would remove this threat by taking Palau, beginning in September, 1944. This invasion would be timed so that MacArthur could "Return" to the Philippines a few months later, relieved of any concern about Palau.

Halsey, Nimitz's most senior Admiral, had a very different view about Palau. Indeed, he opposed the taking of the Island group, arguing that Japan was in retreat everywhere.

All areas near or in the path of MacArthur's planned invasion
route to Leyte, in the nearby Philippines, Halsey argued,
were relatively free of Japanese resistance.[31]

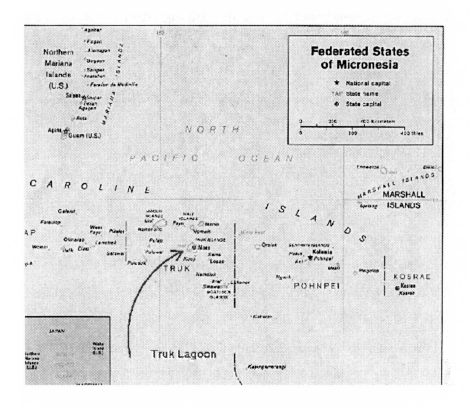

Besides Halsey's strong recommendations, it seemed hardly
necessary for Nimitz to have been reminded that there was
no longer any threat to the Philippine invasion from Truk,
which had been reduced to a hollow shell a few months earlier
by fliers from Task Force 58. Leyte was the first step in the

General's Return, to be followed by landings in Luzon and in the Southern Philippines.

Halsey asked Nimitz, his Fleet Admiral, for authority to move his Third Fleet away from Palau and to steam toward Leyte in support of the invasion there. Nimitz refused, claiming—in an astounding response—that forces were already at sea, and it would be too difficult to recall them.[32]

The "lessons learned" at Tarawa—so claimed the Naval strategists—found no application in this invasion. Peleliu, unlike the Tarawa atoll, was not flat and level, despite the incredible insistence of intelligence analysts that it was.[33] Aircraft reconnaissance surely must have shown otherwise. Indeed, Peleliu is hilly in large part; the Umbrogal Mountains dominate the landscape. These features allowed the Japanese to use caves, jungles and coral ridges, combined with the construction of bunkers and tunnels, to create a virtually impregnable defense. Obviously, the Japanese had learned well the lessons of Tarawa. Unlike at Tarawa, for example, the Japanese held their gunfire while the approaching landing craft were far away at sea, thus not revealing their defensive positions to the U.S. Naval gunners. The Japanese defenses were thereby left virtually untouched, which meant that most advances by U.S. forces exacted a bloody toll upon the attackers. There were no Banzai charges. Rather, it would be from untouched tunnels, caves and bunkers, often at night, that the Japanese organized their stealthy attacks upon the U.S. positions with devastating results.

Day after day, in the stifling heat and humidity of this equatorial island, U.S. casualties continued to mount, with U.S. attackers suffering far greater numbers than the defenders. The formidable Japanese defenses and the tenacious defenders represented one major obstacle. The other—and more important—obstacle was the stubborn insistence of the commanding Marine General William H. Rupertus that his Marines needed no assistance from the 81st Army Division, waiting nearby for the call to help. The General's hubris was reflected in his repeated claims that the war would be over shortly, this despite the staggering losses to the General's over-extended Marines.[34] Only after the General was ordered to do so by his corps commander, did he allow the 81st Division to join in the battle. There is no doubt that the General's arrogance, especially his vain belief that his Marines could win any battle against these sub-human Japs, played a large part in making Peleliu the battlefield with the highest casualty rate of all of the battles in the Pacific War.

Was the battle for Palau worth it? Did the U.S. victory there figure in any significant way in the ultimate victory over Japan? Was it instrumental in MacArthur's Return to the Philippines? Could any material, important facts be cited in favor of the battle for Palau? This author has examined the historical record dealing with this tragic adventure, where the combatants suffered 21,683 casualties; more than half of them were killed. Not one military historian who has studied the battle has offered any credible rationale for the invasion of Palau.[35] Indeed, it may be equally difficult to understand why the Japanese put up such a fanatical defense for an inconsequential island group—one having no strategic value in the defense of their Home Islands. As would become clear in subsequent invasions, however, the Japanese High Command had by then decided that victory was no longer possible. The price for each U.S. advance, accordingly, would be a heavy toll of American lives.

So we have the tragedy of Palau which, like many wars mankind has fought through the ages, relied on faulty information. Not only was this battle based on a flawed strategy, but it was also frequently dominated by the hubris of a General Rupertis and by the stiff-necked posture of an Admiral Nimitz who was not willing to cancel a questionable campaign because "it would be too difficult" to call it off. Palau, a "forgotten war in a remote battlefield," as one writer has called it, has now become a "paradise" for scuba divers and honeymooners.

The Winter Soldiers— Iwo Jima

The summer soldier and the sunshine patriot will,
in this crisis, shrink from the service of his country.
But he that stands it now deserves the love
and thanks of man and woman.
—*Tom Paine*

WHO IS NOT STIRRED emotionally when viewing that great statue of the flag being raised on Mt. Suribachi, or by Joe Rosenthal's dramatic photograph? Try to sense those desperate moments and try to feel how the Marines of Fox and Easy Companies felt while crouching in foxholes on the slope of Suribachi, when they were ordered to advance to the mountain top to plant the colors—you and you and you and you. It was probably a wordless procession; nothing needed to be said as the flagstaff was tilted upright and then thrust into the shifting volcanic soil. Besides, it was an achingly visceral fear that each Marine was feeling now, knowing during the ascent that his whole body was exposed to enemy gunfire. Each had steeled himself against the shock of a bullet tearing into his guts from a Japanese sniper. It's not difficult to envision the Japanese defenders leaving one of the many tunnels on Suribachi as the Marines advanced up the mountain.

Then along came Joe Rosenthal, who knew a great photo idea when he saw it. "Why not?" probably was the reaction of the Marines and the Navy Corpsman.

These Marines of Fox and Easy Company preceded the "six" in the Rosenthal photograph.

They agreed to let Rosenthal take a couple of photos, now exposing all of them to enemy gunfire. All six would survive the flag raising, but three would die before victory.[36]

Of the 70,000 Marines who attacked Iwo Jima, starting on February 16, 1945, 7,000 would die and 19,000 would be wounded.[37] Almost four of every ten Marines—not including those who would survive with post-traumatic shock—were either killed or wounded. Iwo Jima would not be secured until more than a month later, despite the prediction by Marine

General Julian Smith that the island would be taken in ten days.[38] By then, there would be twenty-seven Congressional Medals of Honor awarded to the Marines who took part. That's more than a quarter of all the Congressional Medals given to the Marine Corps during World War II.[39] Admiral Nimitz said, "Among the men who fought on Iwo Jima, uncommon valor was a common virtue." In Tom Paine's ringing phrase, the Marines at Iwo Jima were not "summer soldiers." The island's defenders fought virtually to the end, with 1,083 of the original 22,000 captured. The rest were killed.[40]

Mt. Suribachi in the distance

As had been decided earlier at Palau, no longer was there any hope for victory for the Japanese. The battle plan for General Kuribayashi, the Iwo Jima Commander, called for "a gradual depletion of the enemy's attack forces." He told his troops, "Even if the situation gets out of hand, defend a corner of the island to the death!" Another order exhorted his soldiers to "kill ten of the enemy before dying." In one of his last letters to his wife, the General told her, "Do not look for my return."[41]

With such fanatical Japanese defenses, here and in earlier battles, there may be grounds for speculating that at least some among the Japanese High Command believed that, with the mounting American bloodbaths, America would settle for something less than complete victory. If this belief had been entertained, it would have grossly underestimated the deep well of hatred many Americans harbored toward Japan, even to the extent of accepting increasingly heavy losses in the Pacific War, almost anything to bring Japan to its knees.

The Japanese nevertheless had learned well from the Palau battle a year earlier how to improve upon the defenses that were formidable even there.[42] They would increase the labyrinth of tunnels and caves on Iwo Jima. This time, the Japanese mixed the island's abundant volcanic ash with cement, producing reinforced concrete from which they created pillboxes, blockhouses, and command centers, many with walls four feet thick.[43] These structures were common throughout the island. Again, as at Palau, there would be no suicide Banzai charges. Attacks upon Marines would be done at night—also like at Palau—from the rabbit warren of tunnels all over the island. Finally, like at Palau, there would be no firing upon the approaching Higgins boats and LVTs, as this might disclose gun positions.[44]

The important question to ask now was: What had the U.S. commanders learned from Palau? From Guam? From Saipan? Once the decision was made to attack Iwo Jima, was there any evidence that a thorough review of landing tactics had been undertaken? In all amphibious assaults before this one, U.S. forces had always landed in direct, massive attacks on the beaches. "Operation Detachment" would be no different. The assault on Iwo Jima called for direct frontal assault on this island's 3,000 yards of beaches.[45] Would one or more diversionary landings have tricked the Japanese into revealing a number of their gun positions? What alternative weapons might have been equally or more effective? Would intensive aerial reconnaissance have been successful in finding weaknesses in Japanese defenses? Would a series of small-scale probing attacks have helped pinpoint major gun positions? Would they have uncovered command centers? Marine General Holland Smith had urged sustained heavy Naval bombardment prior to the landings. When considering the high esteem in which Smith was held by his fellow senior officers, it seems incredible that his advice was completely ignored. If any of the foregoing essential strategies had been used, and found to forewarn disaster, then those in command at least would have had the critically needed information to decide whether to go forward despite the cost. Or would they abandon the "Bonin ladder" strategy toward Japan? (Iwo Jima is one of the Bonin Islands). There is no record showing that any of the choices outlined above had even been considered. Plan "B" or "C", if either was developed, has never come to light. Tragically, the horrors of Palau would be repeated at Iwo Jima, except that there would be twice as many casualties this time, and three times more deaths.

The reasons for the battle of Iwo Jima may be summarized: B-29s going to or returning from bombing runs on Japan could use the island as an emergency landing strip.[46] The new air base would also allow the stationing of long-range P-51s to escort the B-29s, guarding them against Japanese fighter planes while over Japan's skies. Iwo Jima's conquest was hailed as evidence of America's steady advance to Japan.

About the B-29s: This notoriously trouble-plagued plane seemingly was in constant need of an emergency landing site. But was a speck of island 4.5 miles long and 2.5 miles wide in the vastness of the Pacific an appropriate site? Was the long-range P-51 really needed to escort the B-29s—a pressurized plane with a ceiling of 33,000 feet, an airspeed of 350 mph, and state-of-the-art guns?[47] This speed and ceiling was far beyond the capabilities of all but a few of the Japanese planes of that period, and those few needed to be stripped down in order to reach the B-29s at an altitude of five miles. Even so, the interceptors could stay aloft only for a short time. Only the heaviest Japanese anti-aircraft guns were effective against the B-29 onslaughts. How did the cruel arithmetic of battles finally work out? According to one report, in a zero-sum game gone awry, 2,400 B-29s did in fact put down on Iwo Jima. With eleven crew members per plane, that meant that the lives of 27,000 air crew members were saved. Thus, there was a net gain of 21,000 lives—after deducting the 7,000 Marine dead—assuming that the 17,000 wounded Marines were able to resume normal lives afterward, and ignoring altogether the post-traumatic syndrome of all survivors.

The pilots of the 2,400 planes that found a safe haven in Iwo Jima is, by itself, significant. This was an incredible number of planes that were in urgent need of help. The 2,400 crippled or otherwise disabled B-29s need to be viewed in the light of the 3,000+ mile round trip involved between Tinian and Japan. Given the history of this lousy plane, many air crews must have died in the Pacific, far from Iwo Jima or their home bases. In these instances, they were following the advice of their Commanding Air Force General LeMay to ditch at sea in the obviously forlorn hope of "being picked up by rescue submarines" rather than run the risk of being "killed outright by Japanese civilians."[48] Of the 371 bombers that were reported lost, there is no record of the number that were lost at sea.

Besides saving the lives of a number of B-29 air crews, all that can be said about the conquest of Iwo Jima is that it was a symbolic victory. This was the first time Japanese soil was taken by one of its enemies in thousands of years. Beyond this, did the killing of 21,000 Japanese defenders on an insignificant island represent an important factor in that war? Rabaul, Truk, and other island redoubts had been bypassed and left to wither on the vine. Was Iwo Jima really a special case? It is highly problematical to claim that it was instrumental in the ultimate defeat of Japan, especially if there had not been an atomic bomb. In the final analysis, there were too many unwarranted assumptions, too many risky projections, and most important, despite the recent Palau experience, an incredible unwillingness by the area Commanders to adopt alternative battle plans. This is especially true of those in command who recklessly and seemingly, deliberately, exposed the attacking Marines to death and wounds. The inescapable conclusion is that a flawed plane was responsible for a flawed strategy, resulting in the tragic loss of American lives, the many wounded, and—too often ignored in calculating the toll of battle—post-traumatic syndrome, no doubt, of thousands more. The nightmare of Palau, which produced these traumatic shocks, would be compounded for those who survived Iwo Jima.

In sum, there are many who contributed to the sad legacy of Iwo Jima: the Boeing Company, which delivered untested planes to the air crews who would fly them; the U.S. Air Force whose procurement agents were complicit in the "make ready" manufacturing of these planes, as will be explained in Chapter Five; to those in command who deemed the taking of Iwo Jima to be essential in the defeat of Japan, while ordering a direct, frontal assault on an island they knew to be heavily defended against such assaults.

General MacArthur and Politics—Return To The Philippines

Such are thou and I; but what I am thou
canst not be; what thou art any one of
the multitude may be.
—*Marcus Valerius Martial*

"WE MUST BE CAREFUL not to allow our personal feelings and Philippines political considerations to override our great objective, which is the early conclusion of the war with Japan," cautioned General George Marshall in a June, 1944 memo to General MacArthur.[49] There was another reason Marshall wanted to silence MacArthur's rhetorical bombasts about his "Return." The Joint Chiefs had decided early in the war to bypass the Philippines.[50]

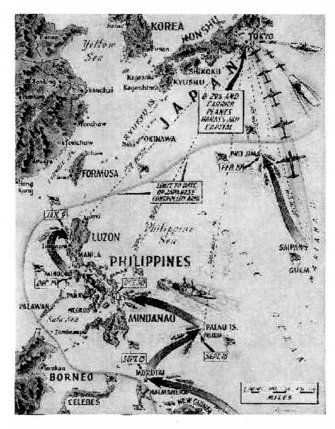

The Philippines, including both the Northern and Southern Philippines

Leyte, in the Northern Philippines

The Joint Chiefs, under Marshall, had decided that the taking of the Philippines was not needed as the essential prelude to victory over Japan. Almost three years would elapse between the Pearl Harbor attack and the invasion of the Philippines in October, 1944. During much of that time, Marshall and MacArthur were constantly at odds with each other on the basic strategy that would lead to Japan's defeat. Marshall's great objective was always to defeat Japan "with the fewest American casualties."[51] Marshall wanted a free hand in deciding which battles would be fought that would be consistent with his great objective. To Marshall, always the soldier, politics was distasteful and unrelated to winning battles.

MacArthur's arguments in favor of the Return were blatantly political and emotional as well. "To defeat Japan before liberating the Philippines," wrote Admiral Morison, quoting MacArthur, "would be as monstrous as having General deGaulle defeat Germany before liberating France."[52]

"If we failed the Filipino," said MacArthur, continuing his theatrics, "no Asiatic would trust us." Finally, "We are absolutely honor-bound to liberate the Philippines." MacArthur's fustian raving, along with his perennial threats to resign, must have been tiresome for the stolid Marshall to read or to listen to with almost every contact between the two Generals, but Marshall was unyielding until something really "political" began to develop.

The really *political* arose when FDR, late in his third term in office, decided to run for another term. MacArthur's many threats to resign would be taken seriously this time by an ailing FDR. Both the President and Marshall were well aware that MacArthur was being urged by Roosevelt-haters back home to seek the Republican Party nomination.[53] Both also knew that the President's enfeebled condition would be a major factor in the election campaign, possibly leading to MacArthur gaining the Presidency. Besides, an ego-driven

FDR could not possibly consider anybody but himself in the office of the Presidency, especially MacArthur. (FDR would be re-elected, but would die before the end of the first year of his fourth term.) For that reason, as Marshall had feared, FDR would overrule Marshall. After FDR returned from a series of meetings in Hawaii with Nimitz and MacArthur, he gave a radio broadcast from the White House in which he declared simply that he was "in complete accord with my old friend, General MacArthur."[54] (The President didn't declare what the "accord" was.) Marshall now had no choice but to endorse MacArthur's strategy. Although it took him another month of foot-dragging, he finally did, with one restriction.

Marshall, through the Joint Chiefs, gave MacArthur authorization to invade Leyte, Luzon, and other islands in the Northern Philippines—the population and cultural center of the Philippines—but not those in the Southern Philippines. MacArthur, nevertheless, attacked Mindanao and other islands in the South because it was, as MacArthur called it, "for the common cause."[55]

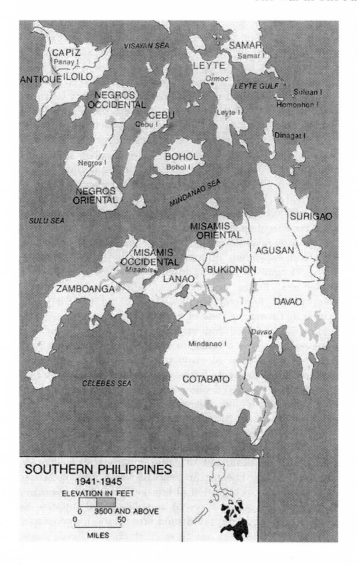

SOUTHERN PHILIPPINES
1941-1945
ELEVATION IN FEET

0   3500 AND ABOVE
0   50
       MILES

The "Common Cause" was nothing more than MacArthur's
well-known vainglory. Beyond allowing the General to satisfy
his overweening pride, was there any reason to undertake
Operation Victor V, as the Southern Philippines campaign
would be called? Would victory in the South, with 9,000

U.S. casualties, prove to have been instrumental in the defeat of Japan? The answer would certainly be "no" in any balanced view of the military situation at that time. Indeed, the Japanese rout of the Philippines was virtually complete with the retaking of Manila and Corregidor in January, 1945. Operation Victor V nevertheless got underway in April, 1945. Even at the time it must have seemed abundantly clear to all in command that the Southern Campaign had virtually nothing to do with the Return. The Southern Islands could have been bypassed, allowing Japanese forces there to wither on the vine, cut off from their supply route. Victory in all of the Philippines would ultimately have taken place even without Japan's surrender.

General Marshall failed to take effective action to guard against the *politics* of the Philippines campaign; incredibly, he even neglected to order MacArthur to call off Operation Victor V. Although FDR's order was given somewhat obliquely, the soldier Marshall never would have disobeyed his Commander in Chief. It appears he also failed to sufficiently recognize MacArthur's unbounded arrogance and the effect it would have upon a President who wanted to remain in office. As it finally turned out, MacArthur's Return would result in 170,000 American casualties, for both the Northern and Southern Philippines.

The B-29—
Killing City Dwellers

A wounded deer leaps highest,
I've heard the hunter tell.
—Emily Dickinson

HITLER'S CRUEL LEGACY INCLUDES many bloody strategies, not the least of which was the "Terror Bombing" of cities—a strategy whose objective was to destroy the will of the populace, forcing their governments to accept surrender terms. The Final Solution would kill millions of Jews, Poles, Russians, Gypsies, and all other *non-Aryans*. Germany's aerial savagery would kill many thousands in England and in other European cities. The British and American Air Forces would exact revenge by their own brand of aerial murder. London, Liverpool, Coventry would be busted by the German Air Force. In return, the British and American

Air Forces would virtually level Berlin, Hamburg, Dresden, and other German cities.

Upon learning of the firebombing of Dresden, Churchill said the objective was "to make the enemy burn and bleed in every way." These attacks would also prove to have a disastrous effect upon Great Britain, not to mention the United States. According to one source, "the British Bomber Command lost 55,573 of their air crews, representing Britain's most able and technologically proficient men.[56] This was an even greater slaughter of the nation's elite than the British had endured during the First World War."

As for the war with Japan, from the very beginning FDR wanted Tokyo destroyed from the air.[57] It was this objective that set off a series of battles that resulted in the taking of the Mariana Islands, including Guam, Saipan and Tinian.[58] All of these actions were predicated upon using the Boeing B-29

Superfortress to fulfill FDR's goal. The Marianas were within the bomber's range to Japan. Boeing's now acknowledged success with its B-17 Flying Fortress gave the U.S. Air Force confidence that the company would come up with an equally successful plane that would conquer the vast distances in the Pacific Theatre. Its pressurized cabin, a first among planes of that time, provided the plane's air crews relative comfort during the long hours aloft.

The first B-29 prototype, built in 1939, was a bad omen; it crashed, killing the crew and several ground personnel.[59] President Roosevelt was among the many who wanted to end the program right then, but Air Force General Henry ("Hap") Arnold's judgment prevailed; he had viewed the B-29 as his pet project. Another prototype model, produced in 1940, was deemed satisfactory. Boeing was now on a fast

track. The Air Force ordered 250 planes even before testing
had been completed; the purchase order arrived at Boeing in
late 1941 before the first B-29 production model would fly
in 1942. In order to make sure that nothing would interfere
with factory operations, the Air Force set up Modification
Centers in several locations around the country so that
changes, including extensive rebuilds, could be made to
the planes when delivered to the Centers.[60] They were then
flown to staging areas for delivery to flight crews. The Air
Force itself was now complicit in the disastrous engineering
decisions involving the plane.

Predictably, the B-29 was a trouble-plagued plane and
would be so throughout the War. There were rudder control
problems. Improperly placed cowl flaps caused flutter and
vibrations at certain air speeds. The gunner station blisters
would sometimes blow out when the planes were pressurized
at high altitudes. But most serious were the "runaway"
engines which overheated, causing fires to break out in
one or more of the engines, destroying the integrity of the
wing assembly.[61] (In an extraordinary lapse of design, the
engine crankcases of early models were made of a flammable
magnesium alloy.) The B-29 problems were the subject of
investigation by Senator Truman, then chairman of the
committee organized to investigate waste and inefficiencies
in the war effort. The committee determined that the engine
manufacturer, Wright Aeronautical, "was at fault for letting

quality go by the boards in favor of quantity."[62] (In biting sarcasm, the air crews called it the "wrong" engine.) In an ironic twist, President Truman would order B-29s to bomb Hiroshima and Nagasaki.

Another company would be selected later to manufacture a different, much improved type of engine,[63] too late, incredibly, for the World War II B-29 crews. The Manhattan Project cost almost two ("then year") billion dollars. The final tab for the B-29 was greater.[64] The military's dogged determination to go ahead with the B-29 despite its enormous cost in lives and dollars should have raised a flag for Senator Truman. Was there collusion between the Pentagon procurement agents and the contractor? (Not an unusual problem during wartime.)

When the Japanese took possession of the Burma Road in 1942, the principal supply route to Allied forces in the Pacific/Far Eastern Theatre, an alternate route was needed. The "Hump"—so named because it traversed the Himalayan Mountains—would become the air route for supplying the B-29 bases set up in India and China.[65] It was from these bases in 1944 that the first air strikes against Japan would be made since the Doolittle raid of 1942. The Indian and Chinese bases soon became peripheral, however, to the main bases that were being set up in the Marianas to attack Tokyo, only a few months after those launched from China and India. Given the Marianas decision, it's puzzling why bombing flights to

Japan were being made from the remote locations in China and India as late as 1945.

The question needs to be raised: Why were B-29 bases set up in India and China—with the squandering of resources, especially the almost certain loss of many lives among the air crews flying these long distances in unreliable planes—when it had already been decided that the main bombing effort would come from the Marianas?

A B-29 base in India

An even more basic question is: Was there any serious thought to moving the remote Chinese base in Chengtu to one closer to Japan, and giving up on the invasion of the Marianas? Even though the Japanese had occupied parts of China, there were surely other locations in that huge country that would have been within easy striking distance of Japan. A strategic location in China could have been secured and then defended, probably with no more military effort than was required to take all of the Marianas Islands. If a Chinese base had been set up, the next logical step would have been to use Chinese coastal cities as part of the supply route to the B-29 base. Available records show no evidence that consideration was ever given to any of the foregoing choices.

Another important factor would have come into play with a strategically located Chinese base close to Japan. If the base had been less than 1,000 miles from Tokyo, it would be within the range of the vaunted B-17 Flying Fortress.[66] The other heavy bomber in use in Europe, the B-24, was an equally reliable plane. Both planes would have served well as complements to the B-29, compounding the destruction of Japan's cities, hopefully hastening the day of Japan's surrender.

Despite its faults, the B-29 was the only plane in America's Air Force that had the capability of transporting "Little Boy" and "Fat Man" to Japan.

"Little Boy"

There was no choice, of course, about the means for delivering the fatal weapon; there was only the question of how best to do this, especially with the fewest American casualties. Here again, as I have pointed out elsewhere in this book, America's military commanders demonstrated their inflexibility, their seeming unwillingness to consider alternatives—to have Plan B or Plan C available if Plan A was not found to advance the war effort with the fewest American casualties. Rather, as discussed in Chapter 3, the invasion of Iwo Jima—Plan A, with 26,000 casualties—would be fought primarily because the B-29 was not an airworthy plane. Iwo Jima, it was decided, would be a safe harbor for air crews flying to and returning from Japan. There is no record that any of the alternative courses of action outlined here were considered at the highest levels.

Okinawa and the Manhattan Project

My center is giving way,
my right is in retreat; situation excellent.
I shall attack.
    —*French General Foch, Battle of the Marne*

A REMARKABLE "SECRET" MEMORANDUM, dated September 30, 1944, was delivered to Secretary of War Henry Stimson. (See Appendix "C" for the complete document.) In the memorandum, two distinguished scientists, Vannevar Bush and James Conant, of the Office of Scientific Research and Development—a wartime agency—advised Stimson, "There is every reason to believe that before August 1, 1945, atomic bombs will have been demonstrated ... which means that one B-29 bomber could accomplish with such a bomb the same damage against weak industrial and civilian targets as

100 to 1,000 B-29 bombers." Actually, the successful Trinity Test at Alamogordo would take place, as predicted, on July 16, 1945. (With notable prescience, Bush and Conant also observed that "it would be possible ... for any nation with good technical and scientific resources to reach our present position in three or four years.") The two scientists' judgment was not based on mere speculation. Bush and Conant were in virtual daily contact with General Leslie Groves, the head of the Manhattan Project in New Mexico. Both scientists also had a personal relationship of long standing with Robert Oppenheimer, the General's chief scientist. Bush and Conant indeed had "every reason" for believing that America would soon have a super-bomb.

The Battle of Okinawa would begin in April, 1945, resulting in 49,000 U.S. casualties. This would be only a few months before the successful test in New Mexico. Japan's Kamikaze flyers would inflict almost 5,000 deaths among U.S. Navy personnel who were on ships in the invasion area, 3,000 more than had been killed at Pearl Harbor. With the loss of lives and more than 400 ships sunk or seriously damaged, this would be the greatest disaster in our Navy's history.[67] The savagery throughout the island would also kill 150,000 Okinawans, a third of the entire Okinawan population.[68]

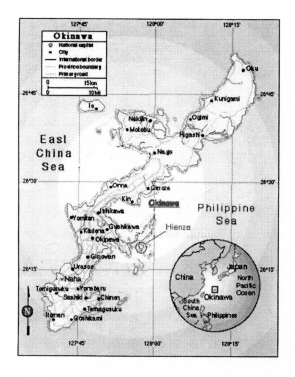

USS Intrepid hit by a Kamikaze

Why wasn't the Okinawa invasion put off for those few months before what later proved to be a successful test? What Bush and Conant knew was shared by all at the highest levels of the civilian and military hierarchies. General Marshall certainly knew before the Hiroshima bombing, and in fact would be asked whether the now proven bomb should be used on a strictly military target or upon a city.[69]

Or, if the battle had already been engaged, the military commanders on the island could have withdrawn troops from advance positions or otherwise have altered battle plans that would have had the effect of significantly reducing U.S. casualties. Similarly, the Navy commanders at the scene could have ordered the ships to steam far away from Okinawa, out of range of the Kamikazes, pending intensive review of the total Pacific War strategy. Both moves, on land and on sea, would have spared many lives. Then too, Hiroshima and Nagasaki, as it turned out, would be bombed in a few months. Incredibly, the Battle for Okinawa would be waged just as if there had never been a Manhattan Project.

The question must be raised: What harm would have been done in the war with Japan if there had been an abandonment or a delay of the attack upon Okinawa, pending the outcome of the Alamogordo test? Similarly, would Japan in its greatly weakened state have initiated any significant, successful offenses against the U.S. anywhere in the Pacific that would have blunted America's drive to victory? The answer to both questions must clearly be "no." If the testing at Alamogordo had turned out to be a failure, Okinawa would still be there, and America's battle plans could have still gone forward with its land, sea and air forces—unfortunately, with the same deadly outcome.

There are no available records to suggest that any consideration was given to alter the battle plans. It would not have been unusual for a planned battle to be called off as, for example, happened when MacArthur was ordered by the Joint Chiefs, literally at the last minute, to abandon his attack upon Kavieng, in New Britain, in 1943.[70] This would not be the case in Okinawa. This tragic situation brings to mind Admiral Nimitz's refusal to call off the invasion of Palau a year earlier because "the forces were already at sea and it would be too difficult to recall them." The bloodshed in Palau would be magnified many times over in Okinawa—all owing to the shameful failure of all in the chain of command—Marshall, Stimson, FDR—to call off or delay the battle of Okinawa.

Epilogue

THE ESTEEMED NAVAL HISTORIAN, Admiral Samuel Morison, writes tellingly of the "strategic fallacy" practiced by those who question the wisdom of battle commanders from "Alexander to Robert E. Lee, who are not in a position to answer back."[71] The fallacy of the "what-ifs," Morison has argued, lies in the questioner's assumption that the opposing battle commanders would have behaved exactly as they did during the first encounter. In fact these commanders would most likely have behaved differently, in a different scenario, causing the fallacy to come around full circle.

I'm in full agreement with the Admiral and have avoided any "what-ifs" in my analysis of the battles in the Pacific War, including the order in which they took place. Indeed, my principal thesis is that there were certain battles that did not significantly figure in America's advance toward Japan's home islands. Serious questions are raised about other battles.

Although several of these events are treated at length in this book, they are repeated briefly here because they sum up the tragedy of needless American casualties, of lives lost in battles that should not have taken place.

There is general agreement among those who have studied the war that Palau was an unmitigated disaster in both planning and execution. Its need was even questioned at the time by Nimitz's most senior Admiral, William Halsey. When Halsey pressed his case, Nimitz's response, "Forces were already at sea and it would be too difficult to recall them," would rank high among the many irresponsible actions taken by America's commanders in the Pacific Theatre. The invasion would go on as planned. It's almost as if the Japanese had laid an enticing trap and the 1st Division Marines were lured into it. This tragic error in judgment cost the Marines almost 11,000 lives.

MacArthur had victory in the Philippines in his grasp with the nearly complete conquest of the Northern Philippines, including Manila. He proceeded, nevertheless, with the attack upon the Southern Philippines simply because he wanted it known that he had Returned everywhere in that archipelago. And this was without authorization from those to whom he was presumably subordinate, including General Marshall and the Joint Chiefs. Were more than 9,000 U.S. casualties necessary in order to satisfy the General's ego for possession of an island group far removed from any significant connection to the defeat of Japan?

There are many baffling questions about the War in the Pacific. One stands out. General Marshall was well aware of the progress being made toward the development of atomic weaponry. He had every reason to believe that the Manhattan Project was on schedule. Yet he authorized the invasion of Okinawa, starting only a few months before the successful test at Alamogordo would take place. In addition to the 54,000 U.S. casualties, 150,000 native Okinawans would die while the bombs were being prepared for striking Hiroshima and Nagasaki. All of that bloodshed would have been spared by a relatively brief, strategic pause in the war. If Alamogordo had been a failure, Okinawa would still be there, allowing America's battle plans to go forward.

Stories are legion about FDR's apparently deliberate stratagem of setting up opposing views among his coterie of advisors in all matters domestic and foreign. This carried over into the military sector where here, also, he allowed a confused, confusing command structure to continue throughout the war in the Pacific, despite the pleas from his commanders, including MacArthur, to name one overall commander. The writer admits his guilt in disregarding Admiral Morison's caveat about the "strategic fallacy," except here the "what-if" doesn't involve Japan's reaction to one Commander-In-Charge, as compared with more than one. But there is no question that there would have been fewer U.S. casualties in the Pacific if FDR had declared who was in command—as he did in Europe.

ABOUT THE APPENDIX

Appendix "A" is a complete listing of all of the 146 U.S. Navy aircraft carriers that saw action during the War in the Pacific.

Appendices "B" and "C", additional wartime documents, are especially noteworthy because of the insights they give into the thinking of those who made the fateful decisions:

"B" is the detailed order, including contingencies, by the Japanese High Command to the Combined Fleet to commence hostilities against the U.S., Great Britain, and Holland.

"C" is the Bush/Conant memo that heralds the Atomic Age.

APPENDIX A*

F

Vital Statistics
of Carrier Types

BUILDING YARDS

ASB	American Shipbuilding Corp.	
BETHQ	Bethlehem, Quincy (Fore River)	
BETHSI	Bethlehem, Staten Island	
CIW	Commercial Iron Works, Portland	
DET	Detroit	
FED	Federal (Kearny)	
ING	Ingalls Shipbuilding, Pascagoula	
K	Kaiser, Vancouver	
LITT	Litton, (formerly Ingalls)	
MINY	Mare Island Navy Yard	

NN	Newport News
NORNY	Norfolk Navy Yard
NYNY	New York Naval Shipyard, Brooklyn Navy Yard
NYSB	New York Shipbuilding Corp., Camden
PHNY	Philadelphia Navy Yard
PSNY	Puget Sound Navy Yard
SEATAC	Seattle-Tacoma Shipbuilding
SUN	Sun Shipbuilding
TODD	Todd Pacific, Tacoma
WILL	Williamette
WP	Western Pipe & Steel, San Francisco

FATES

Acq	acquired
BU	broken up

Ret	returned
Str	stricken
WL	war loss

FLEET CARRIERS

		LD/Launch	Comm	Decomm	Fate
CV 1	Langley	18 Oct 11	7 Apr 13	25 Oct 36	Conv to seaplane tender (AV 3)
	MINY	24 Aug 12	20 Mar 22		21 Apr 37; WL 27 Feb 42
CV 2	Lexington	8 Jan 21	14 Dec 27		WL ~~5 Aug~~ 42 8 May
	BETHQ	3 Oct 25			
CV 3	Saratoga	25 Sep 20	16 Nov 27		Expended at Bikini test, 25 Jul
	NYSB	7 Apr 25			46

* Roger Chesneau, Aircraft Carriers of the World: 1941 to Present, an Illustrated Encyclopedia. Annapolis, MD, Naval Institute Press, 1984.

		LD/Launch	Comm	Decomm	Fate
CV 14	*Ticonderoga*	1 Feb 43	8 May 44	9 Jan 47	CVS 21 Oct 69; SCB–27C; str 16
	NN	7 Feb 44	1 Oct 54	1 Sep 73	Nov 73; BU
CV 15	*Randolph*	10 May 43	9 Oct 44	25 Feb 48	CVS 31 Mar 59; FRAM FY 61; str
	NN	29 Jun 44	1 Jul 53	13 Feb 69	15 Jun 73; BU
CV 16	*Lexington*	15 Jul 41	17 Mar 43	23 Apr 47	SCB–27C; CVS 1 Oct 62; CVT in
	BETHQ	26 Sep 42	1 Sep 55		1982 (still active)
CV 17	*Bunker Hill*	15 Sep 41	24 May 43	Jan 47	Str 1 Nov 66; BU; had been used
	BETHQ	7 Dec 42			as an electronics test ship
CV 18	*Wasp*	18 Mar 42	24 Nov 43	17 Feb 47	CVS 1 Nov 56; FRAM FY 64; str 1
	BETHQ	17 Aug 42	28 Sep 51	1 Jul 72	Jul 72; BU
CV 19	*Hancock*	26 Jan 43	15 Apr 44	9 May 47	SCB–27C; str 31 Jan 76; BU
	BETHQ	24 Jan 44	1 Mar 54	30 Jan 76	
CV 20	*Bennington*	15 Dec 42	6 Aug 44	8 Nov 46	CVS 30 Jun 69; FRAM FY 63
	NYNY	26 Feb 44	30 Nov 51	15 Jan 70	
CV 21	*Boxer*	13 Sep 43	16 Apr 45	1 Dec 69	CVS 15 Nov 55; LPH Jan 59;
	NN	14 Dec 44			FRAM FY 62; str 1 Dec 69; BU
CVL22	*Independence*	1 May 41	14 Jan 43	Jul 46	Bikini test; sunk as target 29 Jan
	NYSB	22 Aug 42			51
CVL23	*Princeton*	2 Jun 41	25 Feb 43		WL 24 Oct 44
	NYSB	18 Oct 42			
CVL24	*Belleau Wood*	11 Aug 41	31 Mar 43	13 Jan 47	French *Bois Belleau* Sep 53–Sep
	NYSB	6 Dec 42			60; str 1 Oct 60; BU
CVL 25	*Cowpens*	17 Nov 41	28 May 43	13 Jan 47	Str 1 Nov 59; BU
	NYSB	17 Jan 43			
CVL 26	*Monterey*	29 Dec 41	17 Jun 43	11 Feb 47	Str 1 Jun 70; BU
	NYSB	28 Feb 43	15 Sep 50	16 Jan 56	
CVL 27	*Langley*	11 Apr 42	31 Aug 43	11 Feb 47	French *Lafayette* Jan 51–Mar 63;
	NYSB	22 May 43			str 63; BU
CVL 28	*Cabot*	16 Mar 42	24 Jul 43	11 Feb 47	Str 1 Nov 59; Spanish *Dedalo* 30
	NYSB	4 Apr 43	27 Oct 48	21 Jan 55	Aug 67
CVL 29	*Bataan*	31 Aug 42	17 Nov 43	11 Feb 47	Str 1 Sep 59; BU
	NYSB	1 Aug 43	13 May 50	9 Apr 54	
CVL 30	*San Jacinto*	26 Oct 42	15 Dec 43	1 Mar 47	Str 1 Jun 79; BU
	NYSB	26 Sep 43			
CV 31	*Bon Homme Richard*	1 Feb 43	26 Nov 44	9 Jan 47	SCB–27C
	NYNY	29 Apr 44	1 Nov 55	2 Jul 71	
CV 32	*Leyte*	21 Feb 44	11 Apr 46	15 May 59	CVS Aug 53; str 1 Jan 69; BU
	NN	23 Aug 45			
CV 33	*Kearsage*	1 Mar 44	2 Mar 46	16 Jun 50	CVS 1 Oct 58; str 1 May 73; BU
	NYNY	5 May 45	1 Mar 52	13 Feb 70	
CV 34	*Oriskany*	1 May 44	25 Sep 50	15 May 76	SCB–27A prototype; steam
	NYNY	13 Oct 45			catapults fitted in SCB–125
					conversion completed 29 May
					59
CV 35	*Reprisal*	1 Jul 44			Cancelled 12 Aug 45 (40% com-
	NYNY	46			plete); hulk used for explosive
					tests beginning 1 Apr 48 in
					Chesapeake Bay; sold Aug 49;
					BU
CV 36	*Antietam*	14 Mar 43	28 Jun 45	8 May 63	Angled deck prototype; CVS 8
	PHNY	20 Aug 44			Aug 53; str 1 May 73; BU

414   APPENDIX F

		LD/Launch	Comm	Decomm	Fate
CVL 49	Wright	21 Aug 44	9 Feb 47	15 Mar 56	Command ship (CC–2) 1963–
	NYSB	1 Sep 45	11 May 63	22 May 70	70; str 1 Dec 77; BU 80
CV 50–55, CVB 56–57					All cancelled Mar 45
CVA 58	United States	18 Apr 49			Cancelled 23 Apr 49
	NN				
CVA 59	Forrestal	14 Jul 52	1 Oct 55		
	NN	11 Dec 54			
CVA 60	Saratoga	16 Dec 52	14 Apr 56		
	NYNY	8 Oct 55			
CVA 61	Ranger	2 Aug 54	10 Aug 57		
	NN	29 Sep 56			
CVA 62	Independence	1 Jul 55	10 Jan 59		
	NYNY	6 Jun 58			
CVA 63	Kitty Hawk	27 Dec 56	29 Apr 61		
	NYSB	21 May 60			
CVA 64	Constellation	14 Sep 59	27 Oct 61		
	NYNY	8 Oct 60			
CVAN 65	Enterprise	4 Feb 58	25 Nov 61		
	NN	24 Sep 60			
CVA 66	America	9 Jan 61	23 Jan 65		
	NN	1 Feb 64			
CVA 67	John F. Kennedy	22 Oct 64	7 Sep 68		
	NN	27 May 67			
CVAN 68	Nimitz	22 Jun 68	3 May 75		
	NN	13 May 72			
CVN 69	Dwight D. Eisenhower	14 Aug 70	18 Oct 77		
	NN	11 Oct 75			
CVN 70	Carl Vinson	11 Oct 75			
	NN	15 Mar 80			
CVN 71	Theodore Roosevelt	31 Oct 81			
	NN				

ESCORT CARRIERS

AVG 1	Long Island	7 Jul 39	2 Jun 41	26 Mar 46	Acq 6 Mar 41; str 12 Apr 46; mer-
	SUN/NN	11 Jan 40			chant ship Nelly (1949)
AVG 2					Reserved for planned conver-
					sion of transport Wakefield (ex-
					Manhattan)
AVG 3					Reserved for planned conver-
					sion of transport Mt. Vernon
					(ex-Washington)
AVG 4					Reserved for planned conver-
					sion of transport West Point
					(ex-America)
AVG 5					Reserved for planned conver-
					sion of liner Kungsholm
ACV 6	Altamaha		15 Nov 42		Acq 31 Oct 42; HMS Battler, 31
	ING	4 Apr 42			Oct 42; ret 12 Feb 46
ACV 7	Barnes		10 Oct 42		Acq 30 Sep 42; HMS attacker 30
	WP	27 Sep 42			Sep 42; ret 5 Jan 46; merchant

		LD/Launch	Comm	Decomm	Fate
ACV 16	Nassau	27 Nov 41	20 Aug 42	28 Oct 46	Acq 1 May 42; str 1 Mar 59; BU
	SEATAC	4 Apr 42			61
ACV 17	St. George		14 Jun 43		Acq 14 Jun 43; HMS Pursuer 11
	ING	18 Jul 42			Jun 43; ret 12 Feb 46; BU
ACV 18	Altamaha	19 Dec 41	15 Sep 42	27 Sep 46	Acq 1 May 42; str 1 Mar 59; BU
	SEATAC	22 May 42			61
ACV 19	Prince William		29 Apr 43		Acq 28 Apr 43; HMS Striker 28
	WP	7 May 42			Apr 43; ret 12 Feb 46; BU
ACV 20	Barnes	19 Jan 42	20 Feb 43	29 Aug 46	Acq 1 May 42; str 1 Mar 59; BU
	SEATAC	22 May 42			59
ACV 21	Block Island	19 Jan 42	8 Mar 43		Acq 1 May 42; WL 29 May 44
	SEATAC	6 Jun 42			
ACV 22	Searcher		8 Apr 43		Acq 27 Jul 42; RN 7 Apr 43; ret
	SEATAC/CIW	20 Jun 42			29 Nov 45; merchant ship
					Capt. Theo (1947)
ACV 23	Breton	25 Feb 42	12 Apr 43	30 Aug 46	Acq 1 May 42; str 6 Aug 71; BU
	SEATAC	27 Jun 42	1 Jul 58		72; aircraft transport 1958–
					71
ACV 24	Ravager		26 Apr 43		Acq 1 May 42; RN 25 Apr 43; ret
	SEATAC/WILL	16 Jul 42			26 Feb 46; merchant ship
					Robin Trent (1948)
ACV 25	Croatan	15 Apr 42	28 Apr 43	20 May 46	Acq 1 May 42; str 15 Sep 70; BU
	SEATAC	1 Aug 42	16 Jun 58	23 Oct 69	71; aircraft transport 1958–
					69
ACV 26	Sangamon	13 Mar 39	25 Aug 42	24 Oct 45	Acq 22 Oct 40 as oiler; str 24 Oct
	FED/NN	4 Nov 39			45; BU 48
ACV 27	Suwannee	3 Jun 38	24 Sep 42	28 Oct 46	Acq 26 Jun 41 as oiler; str 1 Mar
	FED/BETHSI	4 Mar 39			59; BU 62
ACV 28	Chenango	10 Jul 38	19 Sep 42	14 Aug 46	Acq 31 May 41 as oiler; str 1 Mar
	SUN/NORNY	4 Jan 39			59; BU 62
ACV 29	Santee	31 May 38	24 Aug 42	21 Oct 46	Acq 30 Oct 40 as oiler; str 1 Mar
	SUN/PSNY	4 Mar 39			59; BU 60
AVG 30	Charger	19 Jan 40	3 Mar 42	15 Mar 46	Acq 4 Oct 41; str 28 Mar 46; mer-
	SUN	1 Mar 41			chant ship Fairsea (1949)
ACV 31	Prince William	18 May 42	9 Apr 43	29 Aug 46	Str 1 Mar 59; BU 61
	SEATAC/PSNY	23 Aug 42			
CVE 32	Chatham	25 May 42	11 Aug 43		HMS Slinger 11 Aug 43; ret 27
	SEATAC/WILL	19 Sep 42			Feb 46; merchant ship Robin
					Mowbray (1948)
CVE 33	Glacier	9 Jun 42	3 Jul 43		HMS Atheling 31 Jul 43; ret 13
	PSNY	7 Sep 42			Dec 46; merchant ship Roma
					(1950)
CVE 34	Pybus	23 Jun 42	31 May 43		HMS Emperor 6 Aug 43; ret 12
	SEATAC	7 Oct 42			Feb 46; BU
CVE 35	Baffins	18 Jul 42	28 Jun 43		HMS Ameer 19 Jul 43; ret 17 Jan
	SEATAC	18 Oct 42			46; merchant ship Robin Kirk
					(1948)
CVE 36	Bolinas	3 Aug 42	22 Jul 43		HMS Begum 2 Aug 43; ret 4 Jan
	SEATAC	11 Nov 42			46; merchant ship Raki (1948)
CVE 37	Trumpeter	25 Aug 42	4 Aug 43		RN 4 Aug; ret 6 Apr 46; mer-
	CIW	15 Dec 42			chant ship Alblasserdijk (1948)

416   APPENDIX F

		LD/Launch	Comm	Decomm	Fate
CVE 47	Perdido	1 Jan 43	31 Jan 44		HMS *Trouncer* 31 Jan 44; ret !
	CIW	16 Jun 43			Mar 46; merchant ship *Grev-*
					stoke Castle (1949).
CVE 48	Sunset	23 Feb 43	19 Nov 43		HMS *Thane*; torpedoed 15 Jan
	SEATAC	15 Jul 43			45; ret 15 Dec 45; BU
CVE 49	St Andrews	12 Mar 43	7 Dec 43		HMS *Queen* 7 Dec 43; ret 31 Oct
	SEATAC	2 Aug 43			46; merchant ship *Roebia*
					(1948)
CVE 50	St Joseph	25 Mar 43	22 Dec 43		HMS *Ruler* 22 Dec 43; ret 29 Jan
	SEATAC	21 Aug 43			46; BU
CVE 51	St Simon	26 Apr 43	31 Dec 43		HMS *Arbiter* 31 Dec 43; ret 3 Mar
	SEATAC	9 Sep 43			46; merchant ship *Coracero*
					(1948)
CVE 52	Vermillion	10 May 43	20 Jan 44		HMS *Smiter* 20 Jan 44; ret 6 Apr
	SEATAC	27 Sep 43			46; merchant ship *Artillero*
					(1948)
CVE 53	Willapa	21 May 43	5 Feb 44		HMS *Puncher* 2 May 44; RCN
	SEATAC	8 Nov 43			ret 16 Jan 46; merchant ship
					Muncaster Castle (1949)
CVE 54	Winjah	5 Jun 43	21 Feb 44		HMS *Reaper* 18 Feb 44; ret 20
	SEATAC	22 Nov 43			May 46; merchant ship *South*
					Africa Star (1948)
CVE 55	Casablanca	3 Nov 42	8 Jul 43	10 Jun 46	Ex-*Alazon Bay*; str 3 Jul 46; BU
	K	5 Apr 43			47
CVE 56	Liscombe Bay	9 Dec 42	7 Aug 43		WL 24 Nov 43
	K	19 Apr 43			
CVE 57	Anzio	12 Dec 42	27 Aug 43	5 Aug 46	Ex-*Coral Sea*, ex-*Alikula Bay*; str
	K	1 May 43			1 Mar 59; BU 60
CVE 58	Corregidor	17 Dec 42	31 Aug 43	30 Jul 46	Ex-*Anguilla Bay*; str 1 Oct 58; BU
	K	12 May 43	19 May 51	4 Sep 58	60; aircraft transport 1951–8
CVE 59	Mission Bay	28 Dec 42	13 Sep 43	21 Feb 47	Str 1 Sep 58; BU 60
	K	26 May 43			
CVE 60	Guadalcanal	5 Jan 43	25 Sep 43	15 Jul 46	Ex-*Astrolabe*; str 27 May 58; BU
	K	5 Jun 43			60
CVE 61	Manila Bay	15 Jan 43	5 Oct 43	31 Jul 46	Ex-*Bucareli Bay*; str 27 May 58;
	K	10 Jul 43			BU 60
CVE 62	Natoma Bay	17 Jan 43	14 Oct 43	20 May 46	Str 1 Sep 58; BU 60
	K	20 Jul 43			
CVE 63	St Lo	23 Jan 43	23 Oct 43		Ex-*Midway*, ex-*Chapin Bay*; WL
	K	17 Aug 43			25 Oct 44.
CVE 64	Tripoli	1 Feb 43	31 Oct 43	22 May 46	Ex-*Didrickson Bay*; str 1 Feb 59;
	K	2 Sep 43	5 Jan 52	25 Nov 58	BU 60; aircraft transport
					1952–8
CVE 65	Wake Island	6 Feb 43	7 Nov 43	5 Apr 46	Ex-*Dolomi Bay*; str 17 Apr 46;
	K	15 Sep 43			BU Baltimore 47
CVE 66	White Plains	11 Feb 43	15 Nov 43	10 Jul 46	Ex-*Elbour Bay*; str 27 Jun 58; BU

		LD/Launch	Comm	Decomm	Fate
CVE 80	Petrof Bay	15 Oct 43	18 Feb 44	31 Jul 46	Str 27 Jun 58; BU 59
	K	5 Jan 44			
CVE 81	Rudyerd Bay	24 Oct 43	25 Feb 44	11 Jun 46	Str 1 Aug 59; BU 60
	K	12 Jan 44			
CVE 82	Saginaw Bay	1 Nov 43	2 Mar 44	19 Jun 46	Str 1 Aug 59; BU 60
	K	19 Jan 44			
CVE 83	Sargent Bay	8 Nov 43	9 Mar 44	23 Jul 46	Str 27 Jun 58; BU 59
	K	31 Jan 44			
CVE 84	Shamrock Bay	15 Nov 43	15 Mar 44	6 Jul 46	Str 27 Jun 58; BU 59
	K	4 Feb 44			
CVE 85	Shipley Bay	22 Nov 43	21 Mar 44	28 Jun 46	Str 1 Mar 59; BU 61
	K	12 Feb 44			
CVE 86	Sitkoh Bay	23 Nov 43	28 Mar 44	30 Nov 46	Str 1 Apr 60; BU 61; aircraft
	K	19 Feb 44	29 July 50	27 Jul 54	transport 1950–54
CVE 87	Steamer Bay	4 Dec 43	4 Apr 44	1 Jul 46	Str 1 Mar 59; BU 59
	K	26 Feb 44			
CVE 88	Cape Esperance	11 Dec 43	9 Apr 44	22 Aug 46	Ex-Tananek Bay; str 1 Mar 59;
	K	3 Mar 44	5 Aug 50	15 Jan 59	BU 61; aircraft transport 1950–59
CVE 89	Takanis Bay	16 Dec 43	15 Apr 44	1 May 46	Str 1 Aug 59; BU 60
	K	10 Mar 44			
CVE 90	Thetis Bay	22 Dec 43	21 Apr 44	7 Aug 46	CVHA–1, 1 Jul 55; LPH–6, 28
	K	16 Mar 44	20 Jul 56	1 Mar 64	May 59; str 1 Mar 64; BU 66
CVE 91	Makassar Strait	29 Dec 43	27 Apr 44	9 Aug 46	Ex-Ulitaka Bay; str 1 Sep 58; target ship (Pacific Missile Range); grounded on San Nicholas Island (Apr 61) and broke her back
	K	22 Mar 44			
CVE 92	Windham Bay	5 Jan 44	3 May 44	Jan 47	Str 1 Feb 59; BU 61; aircraft
	K	29 Mar 44	31 Oct 51	1959	transport 1951–59
CVE 93	Makin Island	12 Jan 44	9 May 44	19 Apr 46	Ex-Woodcliffe Bay; str 1 Jul 47; BU 47
	K	5 Apr 44			
CVE 94	Lunga Point	19 Jan 44	14 May 44	24 Oct 46	Ex-Alazon Bay; str 1 Apr 60; BU 66
	K	11 Apr 44			
CVE 95	Bismarck Sea	31 Jan 44	20 May 44		WL 21 Feb 45
	K	17 Apr 44			
CVE 96	Salamaua	4 Feb 44	26 May 44	9 May 46	Ex-Anguilla Bay; str 1 Sep 46; BU 47
	K	22 Apr 44			
CVE 97	Hollandia	12 Feb 44	1 Jun 44	17 Jan 47	Ex-Astrolabe Bay; str 1 Apr 60; BU 60
	K	28 Apr 44			
CVE 98	Kwajalein	19 Feb 44	7 Jun 44	16 Aug 46	Ex-Bucareli Bay; str 1 Apr 60; BU 61
	K	4 May 44			
CVE 99	Admiralty Islands	26 Feb 44	13 Jun 44	26 Apr 46	Ex-Chapin Bay; str 8 May 46; BU 47
	K	10 May 44			
CVE 100	Bougainville	3 Mar 44	18 Jun 44	3 Nov 46	Ex-Didrickson Bay; str 1 Jun 60; BU 60
	K	16 May 44			
CVE 101	Mantanikau	10 Mar 44	24 Jun 44	11 Oct	Ex-Dolomi Bay; str 1 Apr 60; BU 60
	K	22 May 44			
CVE 102	Attu	16 Mar 44	30 Jun 44	8 Jun 46	Ex-Elbour Bay; str 3 Jul 46; BU 49
	K	27 May 44			
CVE 103	Roi	22 Mar 44	6 Jul 44	9 May 46	Ex-Alava Bay; str 21 May 46; BU 47
	K	2 Jun 44			
CVE 104	Munda	29 Mar 44	8 Jul 44	13 Sep 46	Ex-Tonowek Bay; str 1 Sep 58;

418   APPENDIX F

		LD/Launch	Comm	Decomm	Fate
CVE 113	*Puget Sound*	12 May 44	18 Jun 45	18 Oct 46	Ex-*Hobart Bay*; str 1 Jun 60; BU
	TODD	30 Nov 44			62
CVE 114	*Rendova*	15 Jun 44	22 Oct 45	27 Jan 50	Ex-*Mosser Bay*; str 1 Apr 71; BU
	TODD/WILL	28 Dec 44	3 Jan 51	30 Jun 55	71
CVE 115	*Bairoko*	25 Jul 44	16 Jul 45	14 Apr 50	Ex-*Portage Bay*; str 1 Apr 60
	TODD	25 Jan 45	12 Sep 50	18 Feb 55	
CVE 116	*Badoeng Strait*	18 Aug 44	14 Nov 45	20 Apr 46	Ex-*San Alberto Bay*; str 1 Dec 70;
	TODD/CIW	15 Feb 45	6 Jan 47	17 May 57	Bu 72
CVE 117	*Saidor*	30 Sep 44	4 Sep 45	12 Sep 47	Ex-*Saltery Bay*; str 1 Dec 70; BU
	TODD	17 Mar 45			71
CVE 118	*Sicily*	23 Oct 44	27 Feb 46	5 Jul 54	Ex-*Sandy Bay*; str 1 Jul 60; BU
	TODD/WILL	14 Apr 45			61
CVE 119	*Point Cruz*	4 Dec 44	16 Oct 45	30 Jun 47	Ex-*Trocadero Bay*; aircraft
	TODD	18 May 45	26 Jul 51	31 Aug 56	transport 1965–69; str 15 Sep
			23 Aug 65	16 Oct 69	70; BU 71
CVE 120	*Mindoro*	2 Jan 45	4 Dec 45	4 Aug 55	Str 1 Dec 59; BU 60
	TODD	27 Jun 45			
CVE 121	*Rabaul*	2 Jan 45	30 Aug 46	30 Aug 46	Completed, not commissioned:
	TODD/CIW	14 Jul 45			str 1 Sep 71; BU 72
CVE 122	*Palau*	19 Feb 45	15 Jan 46	15 Jun 54	Str 1 Apr 60; BU 60
	TODD	6 Aug 45			
CVE 123	*Tinian*	20 Mar 45	30 Jul 46	30 Jul 46	Completed, not commissioned:
	TODD	5 Sep 45			str 1 Jun 70; BU 71
CVE 124	*Bastogne*	2 Apr 45			Suspended 12 Aug 45; BU on slip
	TODD				
CVE 125	*Eniwetok*	20 Apr 45			Suspended 12 Aug 45; BU on slip
	TODD				
CVE 126	*Lingayen*	1 May 45			Suspended 12 Aug 45; BU on slip
	TODD				
CVE 127	*Okinawa*	22 May 45			Suspended 12 Aug 45; BU on slip
	TODD				
CVE 128–139					Cancelled 11 Aug 45

TRAINING CARRIERS

		LD/Launch	Comm	Decomm	Fate
IX 64	*Wolverine*		12 Aug 42	7 Nov 45	Former *Seeandbee*, paddle
	DET	1912			steamer; acq 12 Mar 42; str 28
					Nov 45; BU 47
IX 81	*Sable*		8 Mar 43	7 Nov 43	Former *Greater Buffalo*, paddle
	ASB	1923			steamer; acq 7 Aug 42; str 28
					Nov 45; BU 48

Note: Dates of completion are date of commissioning as converted by the navy; conversions were at Erie Plant, American Shipbuilding Corp., Buffalo.

APPENDIX B

(Only significant sections of the order are reprinted here.)

Top Secret

Combined Fleet Operation Order No 1 [1]

On board the flagship <u>Nagato</u> in Saeki Bay, on 5 November 1941
Commander in Chief of the Combined Fleet Yamamoto, Isoroku

Combined Fleet Order

The operations of the Combined Fleet against the United States, Britain and the Netherlands will be conducted in accordance with the separate volume.

Combined Fleet Top Secret Operational Order No 1 separate volume.

Operations of the Combined Fleet against the United States, Britain and the Netherlands.

PART I.

Operations of the Combined Fleet in the Event War against the United States, Great Britain and the Netherlands begins during the China Operations

CHAPTER I.

Outline of Operations

1. In the east the United States Fleet will be destroyed and United States lines of operation and supply

lines extending toward the Far East will be cut.

2. In the west, British Malaya will be invaded and the Burma route, British lines of operations and supply lines extending toward the east will be cut.

3. The enemy forces in the Orient will be destroyed and enemy bases of operations and areas rich in natural resources will be captured.

4. A structure for sustained warfare will be established by capturing and exploiting strategic points and by strengthening defense.

5. The enemy forces will be intercepted and crushed.

6. Battle successes will be exploited, thereby destroying the morale of the enemy.

(Note: The above outline was generally based on operational policy of the Naval General Staff and, therefore, requires no elaboration. However, the plan to destroy the

80

United States Fleet in the east indicated a strong intention to conduct operations in the Hawaiian area). [2]

---

[2] Notes in parentheses were not in the original notations but were added as explanations for clarity

81

CHAPTER I.

Preparations for War and the Outbreak of War

Section 1. Preparations to Open War

1. In case our Empire decides to complete operational preparations in anticipation of a war with the United States, Britain and the Netherlands, "First Preparations for War" will be issued together with the announcement of the tentative date on which the operation is to be started (Y Day).

Accordingly, each force will act as follows:

a. Without special orders, all fleets units will shift into the new organization and complete battle preparations in accordance with the disposition of forces for First Period Operations of First Phase

Operations and then, as directed by their respective commands, will advance to designated point at a proper time where they will ready themselves for action.

82

b. Each force will take strict precautions against any surprise attack which may be made by the forces of the United States, Britain, or the Netherlands.

c. The commanding officers of each force is authorized to conduct secret reconnaissance only when required especially by the operational situation.

d. Pursuant to defense plans, 4th Fleet will begin to lay mines around the South Sea Islands at the prescribed time.

2. In case the advance forces necessary for carrying out the operations have to advance to the operational areas, "Second Preparations for War" will be issued and each force will act as follows:

83

a. The Submarine Force, Carrier Striking Force, the Commerce Raider Force, the Submarine Group of the Southern Force and the South Seas Force, will depart for the operational area at the time designated by the commanders of the respective forces.

b. All other forces will operate under the command of their respective commanders in conformity with the combat disposition for the outbreak of war.

(Note: By "departure for the operational area" was meant the deployment of forces. It did not mean that permission had been give for use of arms. Operational forces, which were organized in accordance with the disposition of forces determined by the Combined Fleet, were given such designations as Submarine Force, Carrier Striking Force, etcetera, according to their operational missions; therefore, they were different from the forces in the original naval organization.)

3. If the situation requires, certain forces will ordered separately to make necessary preparations for operations. Also, if a great change occurs in the situation , "Second Preparations for War" may be superceded by "First Preparations for War".

(Note: The purpose of the above preparational order was to indicate to each force that its advance to the operational area in accordance with "Second Preparations for War" did not necessarily mean that the force was to commence hostilities. Imperial General

84

Headquarters had unofficially instructed the Combined Fleet to withdraw its forces from the operational waters in case of a successful conclusion of the Japanese-American negotiations which were then under way.)

Section 2. Commencement of Hostilities and the authorized use of arms.

1. The time to open war will be designated as X Day, by the Imperial Order (the order will be given several days in advance). From 0000 hours X Day, hostilities will commence and each force will operate as scheduled.

(Note: Imperial General Headquarters expected that the time for the projected attack on Pearl Harbor would be just after sunrise at Pearl Harbor, 030 hour Tokyo time, on X Day, and that an advance landing force would approach the shore of Malaya much later. Consequently Imperial General Headquarters did not expect that hostilities would be opened immediately after 0000 hours on X Day and even an Imperial General Headquarters Navy Order, which was issued later, roughly stated that X Day was 8 December. The Combined Fleet fixed the time strictly as action could be taken after 0000 hours. Although it was after 0000 hours, X Day, the landing at Kota Bharu was realized earlier than scheduled and was the first battle of the Pacific War.)

2. If case the enemy initiate a serious attack before X Day, the following measures will be taken:

85

a. Forces which are attacked, will counterattack at once. However, offensive counterattack by a base air force before the announcement of X Day will be launched only by Imperial command.

b. After X Day is announced, all forces will open hostilities and begin operations without special orders.

c. Prior to the issuance of the X Day order, the outbreak of war will depend on Imperial command.

3. After "Second Preparations for War" is issued, use of arms is authorized only when it is inevitable, as in the following cases:

a. When vessels or aircraft of the United States, Great Britain, or the Netherlands approach our territorial waters and their movement seems to create a danger.

b. When our forces maneuvering outside our territorial waters are threatened by an aggressive movement of any of the forces of the above-mentioned countries.

CHAPTER III

First Phase Operations

Section 1. Operation policy

1. The Advance Expeditionary Force, the Carrier Striking Force, the South Seas Force, the Northern Force and the Main Force will operate against the United States fleet.

2. The Submarine Force and Carrier Striking Force (Note: Matters pertaining to those forces were left blank in the general order and the details were given only to the forces concerned. The plan was that the Submarine Force and the Carrier Striking Force would launch a surprise attack on the United States Fleet in the Hawaii area at the outbreak of war. This plan to attack Pearl Harbor was kept so secret that it was not revealed to the other forces even in the Combined Fleet.)

The South Seas Force will capture or destroy key points in the vicinity of its assigned area, meanwhile preparing against any enemy fleet operating from the Australian area.

The Northern Force will guard against Soviet moves.

3. The Southern Force, maintaining local superiority, will mop up or annihilate enemy fleets operating in the Philippines, British Malaya and Netherlands East Indies Area. At the same time it will co-operate with the Army as follows:

a. The force will commence operations simultaneously against British Malaya and the Philippines, launching an initial air

87

on surface and air power in these areas and repeating attacks thereafter. The force will also land Army advance forces on strategic points of Malaya, the Philippines and then British Borneo. The Air Force will be advanced to intensify air operations.

b. With the success of the above-mentioned operations, the main body of the Army invasion forces will be landed in the Philippines and then British Malaya, and occupy these areas as quickly as possible.

c. In the early stages of the operations the force will occupy the strategic areas of the Celebes, Dutch Borneo and Southern Sumatra in that order, and, at the opportune time, will occupy the key points of the Moluccas and Timor Island and establish necessary air bases.

d. Immediately after the establishment of the above air bases, the Air Force will advance and neutralize the enemy air power in the Java area. After the enemy air power has been neutralized, the main body of the Army invasion force will land on Java Island and occupy it.

e. After occupying Singapore, this force will capture the key points of northern Sumatra. It will also operate against BURMA at an opportune time and cut off the enemy supply route to China.

4. In case the United States attempts to attack, it will

be intercepted by the main strength for a decisive battle, while the Southern Operations will be conducted temporarily by the 3rd Fleet, and the Southern Expeditionary Fleet.

5. And element (the 24th Converted Cruiser Division) of the Combined Fleet will disrupt enemy surface lanes in the Pacific Ocean and the Indian Oceans at the proper time.

6. Utmost efforts will be exerted to make Thailand and French Indo-China sympathetic to our cause instead of arousing their animosity. Should they become hostile towards us and obstruct our operations, however, armed force will be employed to suppress them.

Section 2. Outline of Operations against the United States fleet

The following are the classification and outline of operations against the United States Fleet:

Each force will operate according to the classification of operations shown on Chart I.

3. Outline of Southern Area Operations

Excepting those operations to be specially carried out in accordance with the operational policy issued by Imperial Navy Directive or by agreement between Commander in Chief of the Combined Fleet and the Commander in Chief of the Southern Area Army the Southern Operations will carried out by the commander of the Southern Force.

Section 4. Operations periods

89

Chart 1
152-07.doc

Page 90

The periods of the first phase operations will be classified as follows. Any shift of period will be by special order.

a. The first period operations

Operations to be executed from the outbreak of war until about the completion of the landing of the main body of the Army invasion for in the Philippines.

b. The second period operations

Operations to be executed from the end of the first period operations until the approximate completion of the landing of the main body of the Army invasion force in British Malaya.

c. The third period operations

Operations to be executed from the end of the second period operations until the Netherlands East Indies are practically occupied.

CHAPTER IV

The Second Phase Operations

Section 1. Operational policy

1. The Advance Expeditionary Force will continue to make reconnaissance raids on the United States and British fleets. These fleets will be attacked by base air forces, carrier air forces, etc., at opportune times.

2. Anglo-American lines of operation and supply lines to the Orient will be severed, and the defenses of strategic areas will be strengthened.

3. Enemy forces in the waters under our control and remnants of the enemy force in occupied strategic areas will be mopped up, in order to secure resources and protect sea lanes.

4. If and when the United States and British fleets attack, take advantage of interior lines and defeat the enemy individually.

5. Intensify operations to disrupt American and British sea lanes of communication.

Section 2. Key points to be Defended and Advance Bases

(Note: Since this section is the same as that shown in operational policy of Imperial General Headquarters, Navy Section, it is omitted.)

Section 3. Areas Designated for Occupation or Destruction

The following areas will be occupied or destroyed as soon as the operational situations permits:

a. Eastern New Guinea, New Britain, Fiji and Samoa areas

b. Aleutians and Midway areas

c. Andaman Islands area

d. Strategic points in the Australia area.

Section 4. Disposition of forces

111

CHAPTER V

Protection of Sea Traffic, Destruction of Enemy Sea Traffic and Mine Warfare.

Section 1. Protect of Surface Lanes

Besides the following plan, surface lanes will be protected in accordance with the direction of each force commander, based on the 1941 Wartime Commerce Protection Plan.

Section 2. Operations to Interrupt Surface Lanes

1. Operational Policy

Operations to interrupt surface lanes will be executed immediately against vital communication lanes of the United States, Britain and the Netherlands. These operations will facilitate the execution of the main

b. The Commerce Raiding Unit will leave the South Seas area at an opportune time, as directed by the commander, and upon the outbreak of war will operate between South and Central America and Australia and along the west coast of South America, to harass surface transportation, and, depending upon the situation, elements will operate between Australia and Africa, and in the Indian Ocean areas.

c. According to the progress of the operations, less than one submarine division of the Submarine Force, as designated by the commander, will maneuver east of Hawaii and off the west coast of Central and North America as long as this action does not hamper the main operations. At the same time, the Hawaii Area Force will engage in interrupting the supply lines to Hawaii whenever opportunity arises.

e. When the First Phase Operations have been completed or when opportunity offers in the course of the operations, commerce raiding will be further strengthened by surface craft and airplanes, and will actively engage in the disruption of sea lanes.

Section 3. Mine warfare

Mine warfare by the Combined Fleet will be performed according tot he following plans and will be directed by the respective force commander:

The main purpose of announcing mine laying is to frighten the enemy. Announcements will be regulated Combined Fleet Headquarters and will be made by Imperial General Headquarters.

121

Appended Chart No 3

CHAPTER VIII

Operations to be performed by Forces Other Than the Combined Fleet

Section 1. Operations of the Forces of Each Naval District and Minor Naval District

1. Strengthen the defenses of strategic points, secure surface traffic and cooperate with the Combined Fleet and the China Area Fleet in executing operations in the districts assigned to each force.

2. In accordance with the change in the situation, advance the air forces and other necessary forces to the areas requiring reinforcement and put these forces under the operational command of the commander in chief of the fleet concerned, or of the commanding officer of the force of the naval district or the minor naval district in that area.

Section 2. Operations of the China Area Fleet

1. Continue operations against China with in the present strength. Destroy the military forces of the United States and Great Britain in China.

2. At the outbreak of war, invade Hongkong with the forces formed around the 2d China Expeditionary Fleet, maintain cooperation with the Army, and destroy the local enemy troops.

3. Strengthen the defenses and fortifications of the occupied areas, secure the sea traffic along the China coast and prevent enemy

140

ships and airplanes from using the China coast.

4. If necessary, cooperate with the Combined Fleet and Southern Army in escorting sea transports of the Army and in protecting assembly points.

141

PART II

Operations of the Combined Fleet in Case War with Russia Begins during the War against the United States, Great Britain, the Netherlands and China

CHAPTER I

Operation Policy

1. The operations against the United States, Great Britain and Holland will be continued in accordance with the operational policy described in Part I.

2. The operational policy against Russia will be as follows:

a. In case war with Russia begins during First Phase Operations:

(1) First assume passive defense, chiefly with the 5th Fleet and Inner Combat Forces, secure the main coastal traffic of the Homeland and protect the strategic areas from enemy air raids.

(2) Thereafter, as far as Southern Operations and the operations against the United States Fleet permit, quickly divert elements of the light forces and the air forces as reinforcements to the operations against Russia.

b. In case war with Russia begins after the conclusion of the First Phase Operations.

(1) Shift the greater part of the 5th Fleet and an element of the light vessel forces to the operations against Russia, and, as soon as possible, destroy the Russian fleet in the Orient in order to gain control of the waters surrounding the Far Eastern territory of Russia.

(2) At the same time, in cooperation with the Army, destroy hostile air forces in the Maritime Province of Siberia and Ussuri Oblast and invade Vladivostok and other strategic points of the Far East.

CHAPTER II

Disposition of Forces.

(Omitted.

143

CHAPTER III

Operations Other Than Those of the Combined Fleet

Section 1. Operations of the Forces of Each Naval District and Minor Naval District

1. The naval stations at Yokosuka, Kure, Sasebo and Maizuru and the minor naval districts at Ominato, Chinaki and Port Arthur particularly will strengthen the defense against Russian submarines and airplanes and will destroy them should they appear in the vicinity of the assigned areas.

2. In case the Outer Combat Forces become actively engaged in operations, the air forces and other necessary forces of naval districts and minor naval districts will be assembled in strategic points and assist in the operations.

Section 2. Operation of the China Area Fleet

APPENDIX C

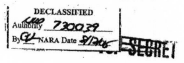

APPENDIX C

September 30, 1944.

MEMORANDUM

To: The Secretary of War

From: V. Bush and J. B. Conant

Subject: Supplementary memorandum giving further details
           concerning military potentialities of atomic
           bombs and the need for international exchange
           of information.

1. *Present military potentialities.* The present schedule
of production should yield sufficient materials during the
spring and summer of 1945 to provide either several bombs each
having the equivalent effect of 10,000 tons of high explosives,
or a correspondingly larger number of bombs each having the
equivalent of 1,000 tons of high explosive. When it is recalled
that each B-29 bomber was designed to carry about 8 tons of high
explosive, it is clear that the military effect of these atomic
bombs is to reduce enormously the number of bombers required to
produce damage to the type of target found in civilian and industrial centers. For example, one 10,000 ton HE equivalent
bomb would produce the same order of effect as 1,000 B-29
bombers carrying full load. If, as seems probable at the outset,
the smaller atomic bombs would be developed, then one B-29 bomber
carrying such a bomb (1,000 ton equivalent HE) would produce the
same damage as 100 B-29 bombers fully equipped. Which of these
two types of bombs comes into use first depends upon certain
technical developments now in progress. It is probable that
the most efficient use of the material from the point of view
of causing the maximum damage for every pound expended would
be through the smaller bombs accurately placed on an industrial
target, which, to repeat, would be the equivalent of 100 B-29
normal loads.

It should be pointed out that these bombs, like all
high explosive bombs, give a maximum of damage when used against
weak targets, that is industrial installations and large collections
of buildings. The protection against them would be underground
installations and heavy concrete structures. Just as in the case
of ordinary high explosive bombs such structures would be relatively
safe even against super bombs unless a direct hit were made, although
in the case of an atomic bomb the definition of a direct hit would
probably include bombs which landed within a few hundred yards.

- 2 -

Although these memoranda are directed to the international situation, we would like to point out again at this time that the manufacture of these atomic bombs and any further experimentation in the whole field of atomic power presents very great hazards to the health of a country unless the experiments are carefully controlled. It is now relatively easy to construct a device which develops atomic energy in the form of heat using relatively small quantities of separated uranium. Such atomic energy machines, which can produce heat but not explosive energy, are known as "water boilers". These small water boilers also produce intense neutron radiation which is fatal to anyone coming within 100 feet or so unless adequate shielding is provided. Furthermore, in the operation of these water boilers radioactive poisons are produced. Clearly such establishments should be allowed only under careful regulation by the government, yet such installations will be of prime importance to the further development of the sciences of physics, chemistry, and biology. It would be unthinkable to prohibit developments of this sort in private laboratories, yet clearly all such experimentation must be carefully supervised and controlled.

A great many industrial companies will want to work in this whole field because there are many applications of the byproducts of this new science. Quite apart from the major development of atomic energy as a source of industrial power industrial concerns will wish to experiment with water boilers and their products, radioactive poisons. Clearly all such developments should be licensed and all patent rights should come to the government. No one can tell what may be the new developments in this field of science, or what will come out of the experiments performed in many different places with these new materials and these new techniques. Results of all such experiments should be made available to the United States Government and, as proposed later, through an international arrangement to the world. As suggested in our earlier memorandum to you, the legislation to control this whole field of experimentation and development, as well as to provide for a national agency for furtherance of the art, might derive its power from an international treaty.

2. Future military potentialities. Two materials are at present in production for use in atomic bombs. One is an isotope of uranium commonly called "25", the other a product of a fission reaction of uranium, a new element known as "49". Both these substances produce energy under certain conditions by the fission of their nuclei into fragments.

THIS PAGE DECLA...

- 3 -

Some of our theoretical physicists believe that it is extremely probable that the energy generated by the fission of the nuclei of "25" and "49" could under certain circumstances produce such a high temperature as to initiate a reaction which has never taken place on this earth, but is closely analogous to the sources of energy of the sun. This reaction involves the transformation of heavy hydrogen into helium. Enormous amounts of energy are released in this reaction. A super bomb using heavy hydrogen (in the form of heavy water) and detonated by an atomic bomb using "25" or "49" would be of a different order of magnitude in its destructive power from an atomic bomb itself. We may therefore designate it as a super-super bomb. While such a possibility lies in the future, it could even happen that a bomb of this type would prove feasible within six months or a year after the first atomic bomb is constructed.

When one considers that such a super-super bomb might be delivered on an enemy target by the principle of a robot bomb or guided missile, or even without this possibility from a bomber coming at night or in overcast guided by modern radar devices, we see how vulnerable would be centers of population in a future war. Unless one proposed to put all one's cities and industrial factories under ground, or one believes that the antiaircraft defenses could guarantee literally that no enemy plane or flying bomb could be over a vulnerable area, every center of the population in the world in the future is at the mercy of the enemy that strikes first.

In painting this lurid picture of the future it is hardly necessary to add, however, that it seems extremely unlikely that any nation would thus destroy large industrial centers or civilian centers unless it was prepared to follow up with air, naval, or land forces. Therefore it seems unnecessary to be disturbed about the possibilities of small countries, particularly countries with little industrial potential, disturbing the peace of the world by secret development of such weapons. The possibility of any major power or former major power undertaking this development, however, seems great indeed.

3. **Present advantage of United States and Great Britain temporary.** The probabilities are great that Germany is not far advanced along the road of development of atomic bombs. It is also extremely unlikely that Russia has as yet had opportunity to carry this subject far. On the other hand,

- 4 -

once the war is over Russia, at least, and possibly Germany
and other countries, could quite easily make up the advantage
which we now possess in technical knowledge and scientific
information. Much that we have found out in the way of basic
facts were just over the horizon when the war came on and
secrecy prevailed. Quite apart from any leakage of information which would be bound to occur if we foolishly attempted
to maintain a secrecy order on our present scientific information, foreign scientists would soon come to the same
scientific point of view as we now hold. Our present advantage
lies entirely in the construction of plants for the manufacture
of materials. Even this could be much more quickly overcome
and at much less cost that at first sight would seem to be
the case. It is an old story in the advance of technology
that after the first person has shown how something can be
done there are soon developed cheaper and easier ways of
accomplishing the same end. Lest we be deluded on this
point by the large sums of money expended by the United
States, we must recall that in order to save time and to
arrive with assurance at our goal, we proceeded to ride
three horses at the same time. We now know that probably
any one of four or five methods could produce material from
which an atomic bomb could be constructed. The erection of
a plant to operate any one of these methods would not be
nearly as costly an undertaking and certainly could be ac-
complished in a few years. We also believe now that the
fundamental basis for the construction of an atomic bomb
from the material presents no great difficulty and the way
that anyone would naturally try to accomplish this end will
succeed. Our present difficulties in this area and our large
expenditures of money and manpower on the ordnance aspects
of the problem are only because we wish to produce as rapidly
as possible bombs using small amounts of material. This requires
difficult experimentation which is not yet complete. The way
through on a more orthodox procedure is now clear and would
not be difficult for anyone to undertake. In short, it now
seems that it is by no means a prohibitively difficult, expensive, or laborious undertaking to construct a plant to
produce atomic bombs. There is the further point that the
basic scientific information would be essentially rediscovered,
if necessary, by another group of scientists starting in the
field when the war is over. The advantage, therefore, that
the United States and Great Britain posses in this area is
very temporary indeed. We cannot overemphasize this point.

- 5 -

4. **Impossibility of maintaining complete secrecy after the war is over.** This point is so obvious that it needs very little further expansion of what was said in our summary memorandum. Only strict censorship of the press or a continuation of the present voluntary arrangement would prevent free discussion of this subject. Furthermore, to attempt to impose complete secrecy would be to interfere seriously with scientific advance in many related fields. It seems to us from every point of view of the greatest importance to have this whole subject out in the open as soon as military conditions allow, so that (a) there may be a public understanding of the dangers, (b) we may have open control by a newly-authorized agency set up by Congress, (c) we may regulate whatever experiments may now be going on without our knowledge in private places, and (d) we may use this new field to advance the sciences of physics, chemistry, and biology including medicine.

5. **Dangers of partial secrecy and international armament race.** As has already been pointed out in this memorandum, certainly the Russian scientists and perhaps the Germans and others may be before long hard in the race of developing this new type of weapon. They could catch up with our present position in the course of three or four years. The danger is that we would never know, if secrecy prevails as between countries, whether indeed this were the case. Hence our own thoughts about using this weapon in a future war might be based on the false premise that our enemies could not retaliate in kind. But more dangerous still are the possibilities of the super atomic bomb referred to in Section 2. The devastating effects of this bomb would be of another order of magnitude from the atomic bomb itself and it would require materials that are readily available. One cannot say with certainty that such a bomb can be constructed, but it seems as probable as was the atomic bomb development when this research was first undertaken by the government. But whether or not this particular line should prove profitable from a military point of view one can be certain that there will be unexpected developments which would increase enormously the effectiveness of atomic energy for destructive purposes.

If we are in a situation in which several powerful countries are proceeding in secret to develop these potentialities we shall be living in a most dangerous world. One need

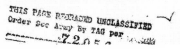

- 6 -

not elaborate on the repercussions of such a situation
on public opinion or on any attempts to develop an association of nations to keep the peace. We should like to
emphasize, however, how closely all these developments
are tied up with advances in physics and chemistry; any
attempt to shroud developments in this country with secrecy
for military reasons would run into innumerable problems
involving various branches of science. By the same token,
however, this subject is by its very nature ideal for free
international exchange of scientific information. And if
there be such free interchange of information anyone will
know fairly clearly what is the status of the armament
situation in so far as this weapon is concerned.

    6. Proposed international exchange of information.
For the reasons already outlined we come to the conclusion
that the safety of the United States and the prospects of
world peace will be furthered by providing for free interchange of scientific information with all countries in the
field of atomic energy. We believe this should not be left
to the usual haphazard methods of scientific publication, but
should be centered in an international office responsible to
an association of nations. The signatories of the treaty
would guarantee that all their scientists would make their
results freely available to the agents of this international
office, who in turn would see that they were given worldwide
publication as fast as they are obtained. The nations in
the association would further agree to allow the agents of
the international office to visit freely within their countries
and discuss all matters of atomic energy with all the scientists,
including the government employees in the country in question.
It appears to us that Russia would be the one most reluctant
to enter into this combination, but since we hold the advantage,
if only temporary, in this art it would seem that the quid pro
quo was evident.

    While we believe that arrangements for free inter-
change of scientific information would be a great step forward
in removing some of the dangers to civilization inherent in
this new development, we believe that arrangements should
proceed further, if not at once, as the second step. The
same international office should provide not only for the
free circulation of its agents among the scientific laboratories
of all countries and the free publication of all the scientific
aspects of the subject of atomic energy, but should also provide

TOP SECRET

- 7 -

for inspection of all technical installations. This presents still greater difficulties and would presumably be violently opposed in this country as well as Russia since it would mean in the last analysis the opening of all industrial plants to officials of an international organization. We believe, however, that if people in this country and in other countries are convinced of the terrific potentialities of the new weapons which now lie just over the horizon they will be willing to provide for such an arrangement with due safeguards to commercial secrets. Since the inspecting agents would be scientific and technical men with the traditions of the professions, we believe there could be developed before long in such an international corps of experts a tradition of integrity and responsibility that would insure that their inspectorial powers would not be abused. That is to say, they would resist the temptation to divulge secret information not in the field in question which they obtained in the course of their duties to their own government or to some commercial concern.

We recognize that even at the scientific level there is some chance for evasion and that at the technical and industrial level there are very great chances for evasion. Nevertheless, we believe that along the path we outline it would be possible to proceed toward a definite goal, and that even if the achievements were far less than ideal the attempt would be worth while. We have been unable to devise any other plan which holds greater possibilities that these new developments can be utilized to promote peace rather than to insure devastating destruction in another war.

(SIGNED) J. B. CONANT

V. BUSH

BIBLIOGRAPHY

About the Internet: Internet sources can be accessed by using either Google or Ask.com. A "binoculars" feature of Ask.com gives a thumbnail preview of the website.

Books

Allen, Donald K., *Tarawa—The Aftermath*. USA, 2001

Costello, John, *The Pacific War, 1941-1945*. New York, 1981

Magazines

Schwarz, Benjamin. "Fire From the Sky", *The Atlantic*, June 2006.

Internet*

Tsushima Strait—Wikipedia

U.S. Foreign Policy—War Plan Orange

Island Hopping—Pacific Theatre

Combined Fleet Operation Order No. 1

Operation Husky

Stan Jersey's Battle of Tarawa—The Japanese Perspective

FDR and Truman, Air Power Journal, Fall 1995

Hyperwar U.S. Navy Ships, 1940-1945

Pacific Naval Battles in World War II

Rabaul-History-Paradise-Fortress

Welcome to Palau

The American Assault on Peleliu

Iwo Jima-The Flag Raisers

Battle of Iwo Jima. Wikipedia

Operation Detachment

B-29 Superfortress-Wikipedia

Boeing B-29 Superfortress, Earl Swinhart

The Icarus Syndrome: The Role of Air Power

B-17 Superfortress-Wikipedia

Battle of Okinawa-Wikipedia

General George Marshall and the Manhattan Project

MacArthur and the Admiralties

* In the Notes to the book, Internet sources are identified by "(Int.)"

NOTES

INTRODUCTION

(Endnotes)

1   Costello, John, The Pacific War, 1941-1945.

2   "...if you come with me..." Ibid, p. 449.

3   "...Admiral Halsey's operations ..." (Int.) West Point Atlas, Asia-
        Pacific Theatre 20. Cartwheel Operations.

4   "...to bypass the Philippines..." Costello, p. 490.

5   "...Roosevelt was relieved..." Ibid, p. 490.

I. WAR PLAN ORANGE

6   "The reason the strait is famous..." (Int.) Tsushima Strait
        – Wikipedia.

7   "War Plan Orange is an American strategy..." (Int.) U.S. Foreign
        Policy – War Plan Orange.

8   "...In case of war with the United States..." See Appendix B

9   "After the battle of Midway..." (Int.) Island Hopping – Pacific
        Theatre.

10   "We're going to steamroller that place..." Costello, p. 428.; "The
        operation was the most meticulously planned..." (Int.) Operation
        Husky; "...the blare of bugles..." Costello, pp. 432-439.

11   "Hundreds of individual firing positions..." Allen, pp. 29-34.

12   "...islands that flanked the Japanese south seas possessions were
        of great interest..."

13   "...I don't see how..." Costello, p. 438.

14   "One million Americans..." Allen, p. 31.

15   "...these frontal attacks..." Costello, p. 449.

16   "From that point on, Nimitz and MacArthur..." (Int.) Island
        Hopping 1942-1945, Pacific Theatre, World War II.

17   "...Rabaul was converted into a veritable fortress..." (Int.)
      Rabaul-History-Paradise, Fortress.

18   "...their F6F Hellcats have just accounted for 17 out of 20..."
      American Heritage Magazine, Cover, Nov. 1998.

19

20   "...we learned to pulverize atolls but now are up against
      mountains..." Costello, 476.

21

22   "...In November 1944, American warplanes began bombing ...
      from the Marianas..." *Air Power Journal*, Fall 1995, "FDR and
      Truman," p. 3.

23   "...In two days of raids...Truk was reduced to near
      uselessness..." (Int.) Destruction of Truk (February 17-18, 1944)
      Pacific War Maps, p. 17.

24

25   See Appendix A: List of U.S. Navy Aircraft Carriers

26   "Landing Ships and Craft: Small Landing Craft" (Int.) Hyper
      War U.S. Navy Ships, 1940-1945.

27   "...The Pacific War was the largest Naval conflict..." (Int.)
      Pacific Naval Battles in World War II.

II. THE KILLING FIELDS--PALAU

28   "Palau is one of the most extraordinary..." (Int.) Welcome to
      Palau.

29   "...the American assault on Peleliu ... had the highest casualty
      rate..." (Int.) The American Assault on Peleliu.

30   "...Nimitz ... ordered the ... invasion..." (Int.) Ibid, p. 1

31   "...Halsey...recommended...that landings in the Palaus be
      canceled..." (Int.) Ibid. (Proven Courage, Slight Reward).

32   "...Nimitz cited the fact that forces were at sea..." (Int.) Ibid.

33   "...Although it was obvious...that the island was not flat and
      level..." (Int.) Ibid.

34   "...Rupertus was still not willing to admit..." (Int.) Bloody
      Beaches: The Marines at Peleliu, by General Gayle, USMC (Ret.)
      "The Assault Continues."

35   "In the end Peleliu itself provided very little…" Op. Cit. Proven
      Courage, Slight Reward.

III. IWO JIMA—THE WINTER SOLDIERS

36   "…Strank, Block and Sousley would die…" (Int.) Iwo Jima—The
      Flag Raisers.
37   "…It cost the Marines 25,000 wounded and 6,000 dead…"
      Costello, p. 547.
38   "…General Smith had predicted…" Ibid. p. 546.
39   "…over a quarter of the Medals of Honor…" (Int.) Battle of Iwo
      Jima, Aftermath; Wikipedia.
40   "…of over 21,700 defenders…" (Int.) Ibid., Final Days of the
      Battle.
41   "…Japanese strategy called for no Japanese survivors…" (Int.)
      The Battle—Japan's Iwo Jima Strategy.
42   "…if they should make for the sea…" Costello, p. 548.
43   "…the black volcanic ash…" (Int.) Battle of Iwo Jima,
      Underground Defenses; Wikipedia.
44   "…In order to prevent discussing…" (Int.) Ibid. Defense
      Planning.
45   "…It was a matter of frontal assault…" (Int.) Operation
      Detachment, The Americans Prepare.
46   "…the only obstacle…" (Int.) Ibid. Introduction.
47   "…general characteristics…" (Int.) B-29 Superfortress,
      Specifications; Wikipedia.
48   "… they should make for the sea…" Costello, p. 548.

IV. GENERAL MACARTHUR AND POLITICS—RETURN TO THE PHILIPPINES

49   "…We must be careful…" Costello, p. 490.
50   "…to bypass the Philippines…" Ibid, p. 490.
51   "…our great objective…" Ibid, p. 490.
52   "…General MacArthur…made the strong emotional…"
53   "…we've sold it…" Costello, p. 493.
54   "…complete accord with my old friend…" Ibid, p. 493.

55 "...without waiting for formal approval..." Ibid., p. 569.

V. THE B-29—KILLING CITY DWELLERS

56 "...The British Bomber Command lost..." Benjamin Schwarz, *The Atlantic*, June 2006, pp. 96-99.

57 "...both FDR and Truman emphasized very clearly to Marshall..." (Int.) FDR and Truman, p. 2

58 "...the Marianas chain of islands were considered ideal bases..." (Int.) Boeing B-29 Superfortress, Chapter 10.

59 "...thus began the long, sometimes tragic journey..." (Int.) Boeing B-29 Superfortress, Earl Swinhart.

60 "...so the Army established Modification Centers..." (Int.) Boeing History-Products-Boeing B-29 Superfortress.

61 "...the most relentless problem..." (Int.) Boeing B-29 Superfortress, Earl Swinhart.

62 "...eventually Senator Harry Truman..." Ibid.,

63 "...the problem would not be fully cured..." (Int.) Book Rags: B-29 Superfortress Summary.

64 "...one of my colleagues expressed astonishment that the B-29 program was more expensive..." (Int.) Carl H. Builder, "The Icarus Syndrome: The Role of Air Power," Transactions Publishers, New Brunswick (USA) and London (UK), 2003, p. 121.

65 "...the last B-29 combat mission from India..." (Int.) B-29 Superfortress, Operational History, Wikipedia.

66 "The Boeing B-17 Flying Fortress was the first mass-produced..." (Int.) B-17 Flying Fortress, Wikipedia.

VI. OKINAWA AND THE MANHATTAN PROJECT

67 "...thirty-four ships had been sunk...including nearly 5,000 Navy dead." (Int.) Battle of Okinawa.

68 "...more than 107,000 Japanese and Okinawan conscripts..." (Int.) Ibid.

69   "...the Manhattan Project...fell under Marshall's chain of
      command..." (Int.) General George Marshall and the Manhattan
      Project.
70   "...they ordered that the Kavieng Plan be cancelled..." (Int.)
      MacArthur and the Admiralty, p. 302.

EPILOGUE

71   "...I should like to warn you..." (int.) Morrison

INDEX

Printed in the United States
86283LV00009BA/149/A